THE LAST BASTION
OF CIVILIZATION
JAPAN 2041

A Scenario Analysis

ANDREW BLENCOWE

978-1-927750-94-0 – Hardcover
978-1-927750-95-7 – eBook
978-0-947480-02-8 – Paperback

Also available in Japanese and German

Published by Hamilton Bay Publishing
publish@HamiltonBayPublishing.com

CONTENTS

PREFACE

THIS IS A WORK OF FICTION. However, all statistics quoted before 2016 are true and accurate. All characters appearing in this work are fictitious. Any resemblance to organizations or real persons, living or dead, is purely coincidental.

●

Change seems to move glacially when observed one day to the next. The opposite is actually the case: the Internet's ubiquitousness: 10 years; making the world's navies obsolete: two days by the *Monitor* and the *Virginia*; the rise of the U.S. car industry from a dream to the largest component of the U.S. GDP: 30 years; the creation of modern Japan in the Early Meiji period: nine years.

The gist of this novel is the inevitable rise of Japan to become the world's sole superpower in the next 25 years. That this idea is considered risible by all—especially by the Japanese—only lends credence to the notion. What will happen in the next 25 years is anyone's guess, but one thing that is sure: it will be very different from what is predicted by current conventional wisdom.

The cornerstone of this proposition is that Western society is heading in the wrong direction, especially regarding the traditional, normal family. In addition to ridiculing the virtues of the traditional family, the West has embraced what is now called "multiculturalism"—a bastard idea if ever there was one. In contrast, Japanese society is beautifully homogenous and pure.

A central difference between the current sole superpower and the superpower predicted here is that for Americans the three most important words are "Me, me, me," whereas for the Japanese the three most important words are—and always have been—"Us, us, us." The Japanese call this the "Power of Harmony."

Another way to view this is to consider this: one American engineer, one Korean engineer and one Japanese engineer are about the same. But ten Japanese engineers in a team always—always—outperform ten American or ten Korean engineers. Why? The Power of Harmony.

Andrew Blencowe
Roppongi Hills, Tokyo
Wednesday, 4 Feb 2015

INTRODUCTION: THE 500-YEAR RULE

PEOPLE FLATTER THEMSELVES BY THINKING they are enlightened, intelligent and unbiased. Truth be told, the opposite is the case.

And this applies to historians as much—or more—than to others. The very act of being a professor lethally limits the ability to dissent and to disagree; today there are so many dogmas that must be accepted in the long, painful, and torturous path to tenure. Even then the slightest slip by making a mild conjecture—women possibly not being naturally inclined to science or that John Keynes being a pedophile affected his thinking—and the massive wrath of the angry priesthood instantly appears like an avenging fiend. The Age of Enlightenment is being extinguished in western universities in precisely the same way the first Dark Ages started—dogma trumping honesty.

It is therefore not surprising that most provocative and challenging books on history are from journalists and other outsiders who do not suffer these suffocating prejudices such as the unequal ratio of female to male angels on the head of a pin as reported in tones of righteous indignation on the front page of the *New York Times*.

And like any dogma, subsequent generations of historians must, *ipso facto*, accept these rules if they hope for a job, just as all economists must accept the Efficient Market Theory regardless of the actual truth.

●

An excellent example of this dogma is the myth of the Good War, which is popular in America and taken as a basis of all history in England. To even discuss the notion that England (in the disguise of "Britain") and America fought on the wrong side in the Second World War is simply heresy. And it is heresy for a simple reason—it destroys all Western historiography since 1945. (The same applies to "the War to End Wars"—just don't mention Belgium's massive and horrific slave empire in Africa—the largest and most brutal in the world; "poor little Belgium" evaporates.)

●

Some people believe that there is too much emphasis on the Holocaust. A recent survey mandated that anyone who agreed with this idea was *ex vi termini* anti-Semitic. Obviously, Israel has very effectively used the

iv

Holocaust as a stick to whip the West, as it has done so since the word "holocaust" started in the early 1970s to mean exclusively the slaughter of Jews. However, there is a far darker side to this conjecture. The Holocaust is used to reinforce the fantasy of the Good War.

The sad truth is that Stalin was by far the greatest mass murderer in European history. While comparing the relative slaughters of millions of innocents is somewhat like mathematicians discussing an infinities of Infinity, Stalin undeniably was far worse that the bitter, hateful Austrian and his cohorts. Thus, England and America fought on the wrong side. This is the reason that America and especially England start and end all discussions of the Second World War with the Holocaust: they must.

●

Just as happened with First World War, the Second started by accident. Then Prime Minister Neville Chamberlain made the horrific mistake of offering an unsupportable guarantee to Poland in the House of Commons at 2:52 p.m. on Friday, 31 March 1939:

> *As the House is aware, certain consultations are now proceeding with other Governments. In order to make perfectly clear the position of His Majesty's Government in*

the meantime before those consultations are concluded, I now have to inform the House that during that period, in the event of any action which clearly threatened Polish independence, and which the Polish Government accordingly considered it vital to resist with their national forces, His Majesty's Government would feel themselves bound at once to lend the Polish Government all support in their power. They have given the Polish Government an assurance to this effect.

I may add that the French Government have authorised me to make it plain that they stand in the same position in this matter as do His Majesty's Government.

Few people realize that Chamberlain was as egotistical and as bombastic as his successor. The above astonishing declaration was made without consulting his cabinet colleagues, as was Chamberlain's practice. The French were horrified they had been lassoed into this madness. (Indeed, when Chamberlain's reedy voice announced that he had started the Second World War on the first Sunday in September 1939, the French were in a panic—in no way did the French want to fight the Germans in 1939, or for that matter at any time.)

The sole reason for one of the most massive political blunders of the 20th Century was the bitterness Chamberlain felt at having been outmaneuvered and made to look a fool after the Munich Conference in September 1938.

When Germany did move against Poland, Britain started the Second World War by declaring war on the specious grounds that Poland's "integrity" had been violated. Britain dragged an extremely reluctant France, kicking and screaming, into the madness. Needless to say, two weeks later when the Russians themselves moved against Poland to take the remaining half not occupied by the Germans, nothing was done. Why? Germany was the enemy—never let the facts destroy a good theory.

●

Closely related to the idea of the "Good War" is the notion of war crimes. War crimes are actually very easy to define: a war crime is a crime against civilians and unarmed soldiers *by the losing side*. Thus Katyn, the huge American death camp at Vosges, the holocausts of Dresden, Tokyo, Hiroshima, and Nagasaki are all ignored as war crimes for the simple reason that these atrocities were committed by the victors—victors: good; losers: evil.

To paraphrase Clausewitz: *history is the continuation of politics by other means*—history is used to reinforce prejudices and falsehoods to make a nation's actions acceptable. The most important part of this idea is the notion of Good and Evil, or more parochially, of good people and bad people.

Thus the Allies of England, America and Russia were the good people and the Germans and Japanese were the bad people. This is not based on any fair and objective analysis but solely on the fact that the Allies won—the winners write the history. (The same can be said for Roosevelt and the last Great Depression—as the statists now completely control the history, Roosevelt is seen as the savior from—rather than the creator of—the Great Depression.)

•

In the Twentieth Century there were four major events: the two wars, Stalin's murders, and the so-called Spanish Flu. (Spain was neutral in both wars and thus avoided the suffocating censorship of the belligerents; Spanish newspapers were the first to report the pandemic, especially as one of the early victims was the King of Spain; in reality the pandemic had nothing to do with Spain.)

In very broad terms the deaths from these two wars, Stalin, and the pandemic were 16, 60, 30, and 70 million people, respectively. So the obvious question is why do the English churn out countless miniseries on the Second World War that are so eagerly consumed, not the least by American viewers? Where are all the miniseries about the pandemic? And why are there none? The answer is simple: there were no "good" and "bad" people—the pandemic was open-minded and completely objective—it killed regardless of country or ideology.

Winners and losers defining Good and Evil are not limited just to the bigoted and dogma-driven Anglo-phonic world—the first chairman of modern China slaughtered over 10 million, but it is the Japanese who are flagellated over the atrocity of Nanking, in spite of Mao killing a thousand times more people. Why? The Japanese lost the Second World War.

●

In the Soviet assault on Berlin, Russian soldiers raped up to two million German women. Some women were raped as many as 60 or 70 times. One British historian called it, *"the greatest phenomenon of mass rape in history"* and concluded that at least 1.4 million defenseless German women were raped in East Prussia, Pomerania and Silesia alone; female deaths due to rape by Russian soldiers was estimated at 240,000. But Stalin's murderous rage must never become a miniseries because it would prove England and America fought the wrong enemy.

●

So what is the solution?

Actually it is very simple—ignore all history written about events that occurred in the past 500 years. Using this simple but effective approach, histories and analyses of the defeat of the Roman legions at the Battle of the Teutoburg Forest in 9 AD can be trusted; the causes of the First World War, just over 100 years ago cannot be. (There is an influential English school of history that is replete with examples of Kaiser Bill's wicked ways. Today—just 100 short years later—all English historians must swear allegiance to this dogma as part of their professional initiation.)

1

THE RISE OF THE JAPANESE SUPER STATE: 2010 TO 2040

By James Jesus Galbraith
Canadian Advanced Projects Research Agency — CAPRA
Wednesday, 16 January 2041

THE POMPOUS AND SMUG ADVICE given to Japan by self-proclaimed Western experts reached its apotheosis thirty years ago around the time of the first phase of what the newspapers of the time called "Abenomics." A great deal has changed since that time—Japan has risen to become the sole superpower.

In the thirty years from 2010 to 2040 Japan's GDP has risen an astounding average of 4.9% per year. The rise has been uneven—the minor recessions of 2021 and 2024 and the major recession of 2029 are three examples where growth all but stopped. Nevertheless, the 4.9% average yearly growth has been overshadowed by an even more surprising development—that the *rate* of growth has been increasing in these three decades: 1.9% in 2010 to 2019; 4.6% in 2020 to 2029; 5.9% in 2030 to 2039. And this growth in Japan has been against a backdrop of an anemic worldwide growth rate of 0.5%.

The now-mute Western "experts" have been at a loss to explain this. The quiet Japanese joke is that they have carefully studied the advice of these western-ers until they perfectly and completely understood the advice, and then proceeded to do the opposite.

An excellent starting point to understand the incandescent Japan growth in the past thirty years is to look at education. While it is a tired old stereotype to describe the Japanese as hardworking, the stereotype is far too simplistic to even merit refuting. And it does not even start to address the real reason.

●

A far more basic—and accurate—cause is the family structure. Just 25 years ago, as recently as 2016, shrill Western commentators were urging the Japanese to have far more women in the work place—to destroy the Japanese woman's traditional role as mother. Laughable as it seems now, these bizarre and pompous ideas were made to make Japan more "progressive"—just like the

West; think of an alcoholic extolling the virtue of binge drinking.

In 2018, the overall illegitimacy in the United States exceeded 50% for the first time, and the illegitimacy rate among blacks exceeded 85%. At the same time, in Japan, the illegitimacy rate was 0.4%. The earlier and seminal Winegarden study was the first to uncover the poisonous relationship between welfare and illegitimacy—that illegitimacy was linked to welfare and welfare was linked to illegitimacy. Starting in the 1960s, the U.S. Federal government did a truly magnificent job of destroying the black family. Not content to stop there it decided that the American white family should be equally devastated.

●

Sociologists and economists have a unique naïveté when it comes to understanding people; for both groups elegant theory always trumps reality—people just get in the way. In contrast, real professions—especially law and medicine—take a far more jaundiced view. Sadly, this second view far more accurately reflects the true nature of the human condition.

So it came as a horrible shock to Western sociologists, safely ensconced in their ivory towers at universities and foundations, to discover that naked self-interest ruled welfare recipients. These people would exploit the ever-growing panoply of payments by having children for the sole purpose of milking the system. It became so severe in the UK that by 2019, over $250 million was being siphoned from the system each day. (This was one of the leading causes of the UK default to the Japanese banks in 2022.)

●

Thirty years ago, one astute observer from the bulwark of the conventional establishment view—Harvard University—pointed out that the affluent American child received over 6,000 hours more "enrichment activity" than the illegitimate child. These so-called enrichment activities were such things as being taken to the park, or zoo, or being read to, or music classes; in essence extra-mural activities; in Japan it is 15,000 hours.

So while the hard-scrabble American single mother readily accepted the fantasies and dogmas of the doyennes of so-called "liberation," the truth—proven by solid numbers—was that the Japanese traditional family was infinitely superior. The Japanese child-rearing by the child's own mother proved to be one of the two driving factors in propelling Japan to being the largest economy in the world, accounting for 21% of the world's GDP in 2040 (the second largest was Germany at 15%.)

One simple example will suffice—Japanese mothers speak over ten million more words to their children before the child reaches the age of four than Western children. Western governments used to endlessly boast about the increases in the amount of money being paid to professional care-givers for young children. The Japanese were mute because it is anathema to Japanese to think of their children being "supervised" by paid help rather than nurtured and loved by their own mothers.

Professor James Murray, professor of child development at Cambridge University recently remarked about being shocked at the way mothers on their bicycles in Tokyo seemed to be always chatting to their children on the bicycles specially designed to carry their children, "it seemed like a private, never ending tutorial of what the young children were observing. The benefits of early cognitive development of this are huge."

●

The second—and equally important—factor for the breathtaking rise of Japan in the years since 2010 is the nation's homogeneity. While it is true today—in 2040—that the average Japanese IQ is 112, this has not always been the case—as recently as 2015, the now-defunct World Bank rankings had the average Japanese IQ as 108. One of the major causes of this significant increase can be seen by noting that the rating of Japan's cohorts have plummeted—the average British adult IQ is now at 94 points, while the average American adult IQ is at an amazing 89 points. (It should be pointed out that the current illegitimacy rates in Britain and America are 55% and 68% respectively; it is currently 0.9% in Japan.)

Of course, education is simply the starting point. The dividends resulting from the Japanese approach can easily be measured by a wide range of metrics, one of the better ones is Nobels—in the decade starting 2030, eight of the ten annual prizes for Physics were awarded to Japanese; another is software and robotics patents—worldwide, 68% were awarded to Japanese firms; nine of the top ten robotics companies are now Japanese.

And the benefits of the Japanese education system does not stop with these metrics; in a new book by Dr. Cameron Bell, *"Intelligence and Social Coherency,"* Bell proves the inverse relationship of national intelligence to the tendency to riot. And Bell goes further to show—using the U.S. as the example—that as a nation's overall IQ declines, so does social coherency;

Bell shows the relationship is more than just linear. As the U.S.'s national IQ dropped from 97 in 2016 to 89 today, the number of riots (defined as disturbances of a crowd of over 100 people) has skyrocketed 56-fold. In the same period, the number of riots in Japan stayed consistent at zero for both periods. Smart People Don't Riot, Stupid People Do Riot.

●

The Japanese authorities are quick to point out that the halving of the crime rate in Japan since 2036 can be largely attributed to the introduction in 2036 of the somewhat controversial Clean And Pure Skin immigration policy—foreigners with any tattoos were banned from entering Japan. There was initially an uproar in the old United Nations in New York over this policy, along with Japan not being granted a permanent seat on the Security Council that led to Japan leaving the UN, almost one hundred years to the day that it left the equally impotent League of Nations.

After the Clean And Pure Skin immigration policy was introduced the Japanese crime rate dropped to an astonishing annual rate of 0.8 crimes per 100,000 people from the previous 9.1 crimes per 100,000 people; the American rate for the same year was 4,512 crimes per 100,000 people.

7

After the success of the Clean And Pure Skin immigration laws, the crackdown on the Nigerian touts that used to infect Roppongi began in earnest. One of the simplest techniques the police used was to record images of people using public telephones that were added around Roppongi Crossing in central Tokyo. (A prerequisite to buy a mobile phone in Japan is a photo id; illegal Nigerian immigrants could never comply.)

This simple expedient provided a raw database of images that were automatically mapped again the criminal record database. Using this approach, an average of a dozen Nigerian criminals were deported daily.

●

At the turn of this century, all Western pundits were universal in their dire predictions of the extinction of the Japanese race. While it is true that the Japanese population has declined from 126 million in 2010 to 96 million today, what these Cassandras all failed to foresee was the radical changes wrought by robotics and the more advanced roboticians. Thirty years ago there was talk of a massive influx of Filipino maids and so-called caregivers. Japan was expected to mimic Hong Kong, where every middle-class family had an amah. But, true to form, the Japanese once again confounded these self-professed Western experts by preferring the

Japanese "roboto-frienda"—Hitachi's advanced range of companions (q.v.); clean, perfect and best of all, speaking perfect Japanese.

Apart from Japan and Germany, wide-spread unemployment—especially for young people under 25—caused massive social unrest in this century. The French riots in 2021 in Lyon where over 900 rioters were killed, or the Detroit meltdown in June, July, August and September of 2025, when the entire center of the city was laid to waste by the 250,000-strong "ultra-gangs," are just two of the more graphic examples of this.

2

R**3: ROBOTS BUILDING ROBOTS BUILDING ROBOTS, A COLLOQUIAL HISTORY

By Harold Faraday
Tokyo School of Economics
Monday, 4 February 2041

IT TOOK JUST SEVEN WEEKS — 42 DAYS — from the discovery of ether as an anesthetic by Boston dentist William Morton to its near universal use in the United States and all the capitals of Europe. The first operation under ether was performed on the October 16 in Boston; by mid-December, the use of ether was ubiquitous. And in the year in question—1846—the fastest means of communications was a letter sent by a mail express train, about 30 miles per hour; six of the seven weeks for the European adoption was the time it took to sail across the Atlantic.

While the adoption of R3 has taken years, rather than weeks, its influence is in the same realm as that of anesthesia. And in both cases, ancient, hoary, and wrong assumptions needed to be revised, and in many cases reversed.

In the case of R3, there were a number of misunderstandings about what is now taught as Basic Robotic Principles.

One of these misunderstandings was the notion that robots were automating manual tasks previously done by people. This basic falsehood meant that so-called "robotic" factories mimicked human factories. As one of the earliest embracers of these privative robotic environments were car factories, it was not unusual to see in the early robotic factories production lines identical to the first production lines of Henry Ford, the sole difference was the replacement of the human workers with robots.

●

While amusing today, this misunderstanding was completely understandable. Examine the engine of a 1903 Rolls Royce Ghost and the strongest impression conveyed is that of a marine engine—the only electricity used was the magneto to fire the spark plugs; all else was gravity feed and copper tubing; even the headlights were acetylene. Change takes time because old ideas that have no relevance to new concepts are bent and twisted in a failed attempt to make them work, as happened in the 1903 Ghost engine. The correct approach is to use a new model of thinking, not twisting the old copper tubing—an automobile engine is not a marine steam engine.

Another critical misunderstanding was at the other end of the "life" cycle—in the first fifty years of robotics, humans were used to build robots. As will be explained shortly, this—like the early primitive "robotic" factory designs—was a major reason for the slowness of adoption of true robots.

Another factor that limited the widespread use of robots was the mentality of both the engineers and of the general public—for a very long time robots were seen as clunky, awkward machines that lumbered around with stiff limbs like a Lon Chaney Frankenstein, slowly turning to view the speaker and themselves speaking with a metallic voice of a "man from Mars." As with most of the advances in robotics, these misunderstandings were first corrected by the Japanese.

A major intellectual step forward was the understanding that robotics were as varied as fashion design—it was not the singular drab green of the Mao Dictatorship or the military hats of the old Soviet Union where all hats were the same size and soldiers were supposed to adapt their heads to fit the hats.

It was the Japanese who first categorized robots into the now-standard Twenty-Four Automata Classes. And it was the Japanese who, in the early 2020s pioneered the also now-standard Twelve Tactile Features. These features evolved from earlier work done at Tokyo University about the functional specification of robotics for home assistance. These specifications were themselves based on the results of teams of post-graduate roboticians, who found that the elderly clients for whom many early robots were designed, complained most about the cold plastic that composed the outer layers of the robots.

Of course, as roboticians were initially trained as engineers 30 years ago, this was to be expected—engineers as a class loved the cold and perfect plastics made by the Japanese Itco Plastics And Engineering company, the leader in robotic plastics.

It was the invention and then the development of the robotic 'skin' of micro-veined tactile synthetic rubber, the so-called 'hot skin' that was the first and the most important breakthrough. The early second-generation housebots, were all covered in this remarkable material. However it did not take long for the clients to complain that the hot skin was too hard and tough—"like touching a warm brick" was a common refrain. So the designers reviewed the complaints lists and then reviewed—of all things—the hibernaculum of the peach-tree borer. It was this concept of suspending the outer hot skin on an underlay as if it were threads that solved the problem. Not unlike a thick foam-rubber underlay over a cold and uninviting concrete floor, the new threaded underlay mimicked actual human skin layers, with a firm outer layer with softer layers beneath. The mechanics of the actual hot skin were very simple—a micro-veined material through which purified water circulated. By matching the room temperature with the housebot's hot skin, the appeal of the housebot was greatly increased. Actually, matching gives the wrong impression; the reality was an inverse correlation was used—in summer the "hot" skin was deliciously cool, while in winter, the "hot" skin lived up to its name. Female clients especially were delighted with the soft, firm, yet gentle feel; many of the late second-generation housebots were optionally equipped with what was euphemistically called the "Dutch Wife" feature for some of the more frisky female clients. (Of course, for the female Japanese clients of these housebots, the anatomical details were the reverse of the traditional "Dutch Wife.")

In retrospect, it is easy to see why the hot skin technology made all the difference—now the housebot *felt* like a real person, just one that did not argue or ever disagreed with the client, and one that spoke fluent Japanese. Interestingly, many clients would manually change the accent from one day to the next (there were 12 Japanese patois supplied). This lead to the development of the different personalities of the housebots, so the client could "invite" different guests to be the client's companion for the day. In addition, different levels of libido could be selected as well.

In addition, the gait algorithms developed by Yokohama University and commercialized by FACOM, enabled the housebots to move with the same varying gait of a human—light years from the stiff-legged Lon Chaney.

It was these natural physical aspects of the housebot that made them so popular.

●

One area of controversy was the software implementation used. In the first-generation and early second-generation housebots, the device was completely self-contained; once purchased and installed, the housebot simply required a regular electrical charge.

Even these early machines required powerful onboard computing. But the later second-generation devices turned the software approach on its head: rather than being freestanding, with powerful onboard computing, these devices were designed to be driven by the central All Nippon Housebot Control Facility—a mouthful for every Internet and Xnet presenter, even when the "ANHCF" abbreviation was used.

However, the benefits were manifest—rather than a free-standing glorified vacuum cleaner with legs, the later second-generation and third-generation house-bots gained the intelligence of large databases and the concomitant computing power of a data center to create intelligent inferences over a cohort-set, almost in real-time.

The benefit of this approach was made clear in the case of the Shanghai Poisoner, Li Wu Dan. This gentleman—for reasons still unknown—laced over 1,000 bottles of Neurosepific, the popular sleep aid, with strychnine. Li had followed Woodward's original approach to synthesize rather than buy the poison; he was eventually captured because of his inability to refrain from boasting about it in the old-style online chat rooms.

Three elderly customers had bought bottles from the same store. And in each of the three cases when the victims started to convulse, the client's house-bot instantly alerted both the ANHCF central facility located in Hokkaido, and also the local Shanghai ambulance service. As the three cases all took place after 10 p.m., the local ambulance service refused to provide the gazetted service, unless an "Overtime Premium" was paid in cash. As the three convulsing victims were hardly in any position to agree, the central Japanese service broadcast a Shanghai-wide distress call. As it happens, all three elderly victims lived after being driven to hospital by a Dane, a German, and a Swede respectively.

But more important still were the messages sent to all 190 other housebots in Shanghai to warn their clients of the dangers of the drug. As it happens, two of the 190 clients were just about to take the poisoned medicine in question.

In some respects, the Shanghai poisoning case was a two-edged sword. Clients were delighted and sales of the housebots soared, not just in Shanghai, but throughout all of the South Confederation of Chinese States. But the Shanghai authorities rightly recognized that the dependency on a foreign power, and a foreign power that had almost taken over the entire country one hundred years earlier, may not be such a good idea.

But with the public acclaim of the Japanese housebots saving Chinese lives in Shanghai, there was little the Chinese authorities dared do. And the presence of a Japanese housebot quickly became the ultimate status symbol among the always-insecure Chinese and especially the status-conscious Shanghainese.

Needless to say, a number of Guangdong-based companies started knocking out fakes in less than a month. This situation also showed the power of central control—each week the Japanese manufacturer simply printed five questions in the local Shanghai newspapers to verbally ask the housebot; the Chinese fakes were dumb.

It was here that the wisdom of the ANHCF become apparent. Yes, the Chinese fakes were typically unreliable and they did break down frequently; but for a simple fashion show for gawking guests, a quick lap or two around the always pokey lounge room was more than sufficient.

But the real benefit of the housebot was not in its manual labor, but rather in its intelligence, an intelligence derived from the ANHCF and the power of the facilities to correlate a massive amount of apparently random data—the case of the Shanghai Poisoner was a simple but perfect example.

●

Also, the telemetry used by the Japanese housebots annoyed not only the Chinese but also the Americans. By using a private and proprietary microwave technology, and moreover, a technology that used 64K block encryption, the Chinese and even more the Americans were furious that they could not snoop. With no ability to spy on the communications, the Americans resorted to a prohibition on the importation and use of Japanese housebots for 13 years starting in 2020. But American households constantly railed against this restriction and finally in 2033 the U.S. government realized that the prohibition was futile.

●

Hot Skin was the second-most important development of the housebot. What trumped Hot Skin in importance was no surprise. It was the development of a completely functioning hand, or as roboticians call it the Hoshibot, named, as it was after Akira Hoshi, the leader of the Yokohama Technical University who spent 19 years developing this unique device.

Hoshi was originally a programmer seconded to this project. Son of a wealthy Tokyo real estate developer, Hoshi was spoiled as a child, and—not surprisingly—turned out be a spoiled brat. However, a near fatal motorcycle accident changed that forever. On hot Saturday night in July 2019, Hoshi was riding his beloved BSA 650 Lightening. At the main intersection at the bottom of Roppongi Hills, he ran a red light and was almost clipped by a taxi making a right turn. In his efforts to avoid the taxi, he was forced to lay down the BSA, which slid and skated across the bitumen into the crowd sitting outside the very large Starbucks.

All this happened in less than four-tenths of a second.

Hoshi tried to stand, but both legs had been shattered as he had hit the white guard rail post. Sadly, he had hit the last of the posts—with a little luck Hoshi would have gotten away with just a little road rash (as happened to his buxom pillion passenger).

As the fates would have it, it as the proverbial blessing...

Being stuck in traction for six weeks gave Hoshi time to reflect. His father added to Hoshi's deep philosophical thoughts by asking,

"What the fuck do you think you were doing, you total fucking moron?"

Hoshi said nothing.

Nevertheless, the profound wisdom of his father's musings did register.

●

Novelists tend to be a peripatetic lot. The reason is simple: new surroundings stimulates the novelist's imagination. David Cornwall, Gore Vidal, and most especially of all, Somerset Maugham; all three travelled incessantly. New restaurants, new sights, new smells, new women, all help the creative process. Scott Fitzgerald's Gatsby novel, written in room 254 of the Ritz Hotel in Paris, is just one more example.

So it was with Hoshi. Not so much the smell of antiseptic and the blandest possible hospital meals, but the quietude of the private hospital room. Laying alone with his thoughts. Assured that his beloved BSA had suffered no more than two bent inlet valves when the engine had over-revved, Hoshi could think. And think he did.

●

His first request was to the private nurse on duty. (Hoshi's father had personally selected the nurses based exclusively on their statuesque proportions—"It's two broken legs, not fucking cancer," his father had bellowed at the manager of the private nursing service.)

"Please bring me an unopened cup of instant noodles, an unopened packet of Norwegian sardines, and a can of Suntory Malts beer."

The buxom nurse was about to complain about the beer when Hoshi said,

"I will not be opening any of these items."

The nurse, who's primary attributes were on her chest and not between her ears, thought it wiser to say nothing and simply to report this oddity to Hoshi's father, who she liked a great deal, not the least because of the father's munificent generosity; for an old fella, the father was surprisingly athletic, the nurse had found.

●

It was this odd series of events back in July 2019 that led—19 years later—to the device the world now calls the "Hoshibot."

The dim-witted but generously proportioned nurse, along with the other two nurses assigned by Hoshi *père,* started to worry about the son. Their concerns evaporated when the father slapped the lead nurse's bottom and exclaimed,

"Fucking perfect. Fucking perfect."

All four nurses politely smiled, even after the father left.

Only two years later did the four start to understand when the son sent them all New Years' cards, thanking them for, as he put it "putting up with what seemed at the time to be a crazy request, bordering on lunacy."

It was true that the four nurses had each—independently—observed the patient staring at the three items on his meal tray for hours at a time. Even when the nurses came in to freshen his room and change his bed linen, he said nothing, staring all the time at the unopened cup of instant noodles, at the can of sardines, and the can of Suntory beer.

"Is he somehow smuggling in drugs?" they asked themselves.

This was instantly dismissed as Hoshi had not gotten a visitor for over four weeks.

●

Once released from hospital, he took the three items to his professor of computer science at Yokohama University.

He carefully put the three items on the professor's desk. Hoshi then slumped into the chair, as his legs were both very painful and terribly weak after six weeks in bed.

"This is the problem for Japan to solve."

Hoshi looked at his professor.

"Explain." was the verbose reply.

"Well these three items represent, in microcosm, precisely what we need to help our friends at Tokyo University.

The professor was well aware of Hoshi's interest in robotics, as it was called at the time.

"Professor, we have been looking through the wrong end of the telescope. Look, we can do the software easily—you yourself have taught me that."

At this the professor gave a wry smile, somewhat doubting the veracity of the assertion. However, he said nothing. Hoshi continued,

"The software is simple to do, but we are missing the bigger picture. What we are failing to see in the nature of the problem. We are analyzing the problem in the wrong way; we are thinking simply in terms of code. What we need to do it to take an extremely high speed film of a human hand opening a can of sardines, and then take it frame by frame. We need to use the ideas of Newton's calculus to slice the action into infinitesimal steps. Then we need to take the same human hand, inject it with local anesthesia, and repeat the process. We compare the two films side-by-side in a split screen, and we have the answer."

The professor said nothing.

Hoshi was about to speak.

The professor waved him to keep mute.

"I hope the government places a plaque at the site of your motorcycle accident in Roppongi Hills."

Hoshi frowned.

"Your concept is bold and imaginative... Wait."

With this command, the professor lifted the telephone handset. In spite—perhaps because—of being one of the computer science professors ranked in the top ten in Japan, the professor was extremely dubious of any form of technology. His dictum was: "*The more enamored with technology a person was, the less they understood technology.*" The height of the truth of this was sales people who insisted on having the very latest toy—like an ageing vampire sucking a young virgin's blood—to mask their complete ignorance: "but this one goes to 11," as the old saying had it.

"Professor Subari, hello, I want to establish a joint project with your people. When? Why, today, of course. I am sending over the team leader I have selected. It is young Hoshi."

There was a pause of implicit disagreement.

"Yes, that's right, his father created the endowment that pays your salary."

The professor's time at Harvard and his learning of the brutal ways of American academia showed in this last statement—no ordinary Japanese professor would ever be so forward, so bold, so crude. But Hoshi secretly thanked his professor for his approach.

●

So started in the most modest and innocuous of ways what was to become Japan's most important invention, protected as it was by 527 separate patents; the machines that built the device were covered by an additional 249 patents.

The Hoshibot became Japan's largest single generator of overseas revenues starting in 2038. Its use was initially limited to housebots, but within two years its use had been extended to over 100 industrial applications. No licenses were granted for local manufacturing, as the manufacturing process was itself proprietary. All countries accepted this, apart from the New China Confederacy. There the various members took their lead from Beijing, which still retained some influence—many would suggest too much influence—because it was the old head of the defunct communist party.

After less than a year, the various members of the "New China" surreptitiously started to import the Japanese-made Hoshibot through the standard ruses of "Foreign Importers." It was like the 55 days in 1900 all over again, just no flying Boxers.

The secret of the Hoshibot was the point raised by Hoshi to his professor—instant feedback was as important as the software. With this idea, the first nine years of the project was dedicated to nanosensors, sensors one-tenth the size of the head of a pin, that fed their information back to the central computers. Needless to say with over ten thousand nanosensors each returning data points at the rate of ten every millisecond, considerable bandwidth was needed.

The first algorithms were extremely crude, even by the programming standards of the day. One of the first breakthroughs on the software side was to change the focus from raw data points to changes in data points. Obvious as it is now, it was the change—the delta—that was needed. If no change occurred in that 100 microsecond data point, the data point could be effectively ignored; instant, implicit data compression.

After 19 years the device was put into production by the three firms of Hitachi, Nippon Electrics And Electronics, and FACOM. A series of impressive public relations events were performed. Amazingly the most powerful of these and the most watched on Xnet was the unofficial one where a blindfolded and naked girl had to tell the difference between three paramours; she had been told two were real men, and one was the newest housebot. Of course, this was false --- all three were housebots, one from each of the three firms.

After an exhausting two hours, with sheets sodden with the girl's perspiration, she ruefully admitted she could not tell the difference. After her blindfolds were removed, she gasped when she recognized, after a few seconds in the darkened room, that all three of her *innamorati* were housebots.

The presidents of the three companies had been watching the experiment live and had a wager that was rather risqué in nature. All three presidents were quietly pleased that they would not have to embarrass themselves.

The three men knew they had struck a new gold when the girl volunteered that she had "never felt such soft hands on my body," and then without prompting asked "Can I do this again tomorrow?"

●

Which brings us to the current state of the art.

It's easy to see how far R3 has progressed from these early days, days when sovereign countries actually thought they could ban housebots, and that such a ban made sense. This lack of vision has often been used as an explanation of the catastrophic decline some countries—in particular the Greater United States—have suffered in the past 25 years.

As touched on above, a major mental obstruction that needed to be overcome was the notion of humans building robots. There is actually a precedent to this and that is in the area of software development. In the early days of software development, programmers would hand-code their programs, first on punch cards, then later from a screen and keyboard. Then some bright spark came up with the idea of having a program to create other programs. In reality, this was a simple and a logical development. In contrast to ether as an anesthetic, this idea took years to become accepted.

A wide range of ever more crazy abbreviations described this type of software technology. One of the better known of these bizarre names was YACC—Yet Another Compiler Compiler. But the seed had been sown, and eventually the roboticians took up the cause.

●

A radical change that was required for the R2 was the rethinking of factories. In olden times, circa 1950, factories were places where things were made, or at least assembled. And these factories had machines and assembly lines firmly bolted to the floor. A worker could leave at 5 p.m. on a Friday afternoon, safe in the knowledge that the factory equipment would be in precisely the same place when he clocked in at 8 a.m. on Monday—the lathes, milling machines, drill presses, and broaching machines would all be there, welcome old friends ready to help out when called upon.

And the same applied to production lines, such as car production lines. Nothing had changed since the early Ford lines, inspired as they were by the Chicago slaughterhouses, just in reverse. The line would still be there on a Monday, firmly bolted to terra firma, simply waiting for the foreman to start the serpentine again for the new week of work.

But with the start of R2, all this changed. Instead of being a fixed and immovable collection of machines, the factory floor became more like a complex multi-dimensional mathematical matrix, where each unit was a cell that could be reprogrammed to any of a multitude of tasks. So the factory of yore was turned upside down—rather than having a machine tool firmly bolted to the floor, the factory itself—as a complete unit—became the machine tool.

It was this intellectual leap that enabled the creation of the first robots that truly deserved the designation of R2.

The confluence of these ideas led to the design revolution that heralded the start of R3. As with programs writing programs, R3 evolved into robots building robots.

●

Hoshi's choices in his quiet hospital room had been inspired—the three objects covered 87% of the domain of work. The sardine can prove to be the most interesting. Early attempts had taken the form of the clever can opener—use a knife to cut the plastic wrapper, and then cut open the can with a rotating disk. While it is true some humans did use a knife on the plastic, most simply tore the plastic as the wrapper was thin and designed to be opened by tearing.

Once torn, the human would use both hands to remove the can from the torn plastic wrapper. Often times a sardine maker would enclose a square of paper that was a small advertisement. These advertisements fooled the early R2 housebots until one of the team had a chance conversation with a blind aunt who had offered the obvious but profound comment, "housebots and I are the same—we cannot see, we can just feel."

The trivial step of closing their eyes helped advance the roboticians' work immensely. Now they felt the top and the bottom of the can to determine if an advertisement was present. Once removed the opening ring of the sardines was now accessible to the housebot. Here, the R3-generation did have a slight leg up—they did not have to risk broken finger nails.

But in keeping with the design tenets, the new generation opened the can of sardines in precisely the way humans did in the high-speed videos. Namely one hand hold the can and the other first pushing the ring back to open the detachable top and then to grasp the ring and pull.

Ever the engineers at heart, the early designers actually had the housebots open the can almost 10 times faster than real people did. As Hoshi patiently explained by asking: "Why?"

The engineers, head in the clouds as always,

"But it's like so cool."

"Forget cool, just do it as *gently* as possible. And I want grandma mimicked perfectly."

Most of the engineers did not understand gently, so Hoshi had to explain: just like people.

3

THE TREATY OF NORTH ASIA: JAPAN AND NORTH KOREA IN MID-CENTURY

By Akiko Akino
Tokyo University, School of Politics
Friday, 1 March 2041

ALTHOUGH SEEN TODAY AS THE HEIGHT of diplomatic normalcy, the love affair between Japan and North Korea was initially a shock to all outside the two countries, and indeed to many inside the two countries.

It was the old monolithic China's increasing belligerence and bloody-mindedness in the early part of this century that prodded North Korea and Japan to become close friends. The old communist party, then based in Beijing, tried to deflect the increasingly violent complaints by the Chinese population about the growing drought and the ubiquitous pollution by conjuring up evil outsiders, as they had done since 1949—"poor China being assaulted by rapacious foreign devils..."

As was to be expected, this started with the Japanese, and a long litany of real or imagined wrongdoings. Any objective comparison with the real evils of the period of 1949 to 1965 where over nineteen million Chinese died at the hands of the communists was obviously left unmentioned.

Unfortunately for the increasingly nervous and frenetic communists, the evil-Japanese storyline did not have the hoped-for longevity. So a different tact was needed, and a junior Enemy Of The People was found in North Korea. The start to this myth was the North Korean claim that Jang Sung-taek was a Chinese agent. While clearly baseless, the fury of the reaction in China was both ill-considered and counter-productive. And this was the seed of the break between these two formerly closest of allies.

Into this volatile mix was added the periodic famine above the 38th Parallel; the famines of 2019 and 2021 were particularly severe—photographs from American spy satellites showed this in graphic detail—peasants eating wood, cannibalism, murders over a cup of millet.

With what now can only be called a breathtaking élan, the Prime Minister of Japan, Mr. Abe met Kim Jong Un in Pyongyang. In a two-hour meeting, the then boy(ish) leader and the Japanese PM nutted out an arrangement that first shocked and then infuriated the rest of the world.

The Chinese were appalled that they could no longer leverage the brutally cold winters to bend the will of the North Koreans by capriciously stopping exports of fuel in the winter months; the Americans were horrified that the Japanese had the temerity to cock a snook at what the Americans considered to be a wonderfully generous defense umbrella, but what the Japanese—rightly—saw as a paternalistic, neo-colonial hodgepodge of contradictory and self-defeating goals, implemented by an often surly and always rude American armed forces increasingly composed of illiterates hopped up on the latest American illegal drug; the South Koreans were the most dumbfounded of all— the whole *raison d'être* of the South's existence was the destruction of the evil North. For the South Koreans, it was particularly galling to see the northern half of Korea proclaim Japan as the great liberator.

●

Always the showman—or as much a showman as any preternaturally modest Japanese could be—Mr. Abe announced the results of the so-called Treaty of North Asia at a hastily convened press conference at Hanada airport. While curious travelers could be seen wheeling their luggage in the background, Abe gave an ad hoc and lengthy explanation of the new treaty. The actual press conference lasted far longer than the actual meeting in Pyongyang. One erudite London financial journalist was heard to remark that Abe's performance was little like a contemporary version of Gladstone's three-hour Irish bill, only longer.

In the press conference, Abe explained how Japan was extending an industrial development loan to the North of nine yearly tranches of 9,000 billion gold Yen per year; Abe had personally selected the gold Yen as the denominating currency to telegraph the message, in no uncertain terms, to both the Chinese and the American of the new state of play.

In addition, Abe had promised the North to "share the technology of Hitachi TeraPower with our close friends in North Korea." This proclamation drew gasps from the more knowledgeable journalists in the audience, as the Hitachi technology—based on superconductivity centering around liquid helium, had been eagerly sought by both the Americans for their wind farms, and the Chinese; the use the Chinese would make of this revolutionary Japanese invention was vague, but if the Americans were so eager for it, as the Chinese reasoned, they themselves would need to have it too.

For the Japanese to provide this technology to North Koreans before the always-loud and strutting Americans and the equally shrill Chinese was an insult of the first order, and everyone knew it.

Of course, the reality was somewhat different: it was true the Japanese installed the grid with its spider-like backbone of TeraPower links, but there was no intellectual property transfer. As Mr. Abe succinctly remarked to a leading opposition member while the two were each enjoying the company of four of the finest Japanese hostesses the Ginza had to offer, "we're giving them the cake, not the ingredients and the receipt." This accurate description, as well as the skill of the ladies, removed all anxiety from the opposing politician.

●

The Hitachi TeraPower was a technology that few outside understood, other than that they wanted it. Even inside Japan, the technology was a closely guarded secret. But leveraging Japan's expertise in technology to political ends made the Treaty of North Asia and the Treaty made a new world order.

4

ENDING THE NORTH CHINA CONFEDERATION'S DROUGHT

By Michio Tanaka
Economic Council of Greater Japan
Thursday, 14 March 2041

EVEN UNDER THE OLD MONOLITHIC CHINA, water was the major problem. It was not water per se, but rather clean and potable water. In 2019, after the southern food riots had been so brutally suppressed, the old communist regime that was then still based in Beijing wrongly thought the worst was over.

But it was a decade later, in 2028, when the year's harvest failed. The ensuring famine in the North recalled images of the Soviet disaster of 1924 and Mao Zedong's horrific famine of 1957. In 2028, the South had made ad hoc and extremely expensive deals with Japan and the Philippines to import staples, mostly rice and fish. It was the South's initiative to makes these impromptu arrangements with foreign countries—strictly against the order of Beijing—that was the first step toward the creation of what is now called the Confederate of Chinese Nations, or CCN for short.

It's useful to remember that two-thirds of all of the old greater China's farm land is in the parched North, and the old communist capital of Beijing's water supply is about the same as that of Saudi Arabia—100 cubic meters of water per person per year.

But it was quality of the water—or more accurately the lack of quality of the water—that caused the second-largest food crisis in modern history. The gist of the problem is that plants refuse to grow, or even continue living when supplied with water that is heavily polluted. So polluted that stretches of the Yellow River would burn for days at a time after being struck by lightning. In addition to the complete lack of water for agriculture, the northern cities had no drinking water. People in rural areas rigged plastic sails to collect rain water; poor people in the cities started to die of thirst or of chemical poisoning.

●

It was at this time that the then-new JAXAPower from Japan became available. Most people forget that the first JAXAPower plants installed outside Japan were installed in the three northern provinces of the CCN. These power plants were a godsend for North China. The first nine were strategically installed on the banks of the Yellow River, near major cities and farms. Adjacent to each JAXAPower station, the Japanese built a desalination plant. As Mr. Kato of the Hitachi corporation would tirelessly explain to each of the curious local government officials, the Yellow River was so polluted that traditional osmosis would not work, and it was simply easier to use standard desalination.

The drawback of the desalination was its very heavy use of electric power, much like smelting aluminum. Prior to JAXAPower, the lack of abundant electric power was often the limiting factor, preventing the use of traditional methods of desalination. As Mr. Kato was to explain, one JAXAPower plant was like having a one-thousandth of all the sun's heat that fell on the Earth, around the clock, day and night.

With this massive electrical source, each of the desalination plants using JAXAPower was able to provide 11 million cubic meters of pure water every day. Taken together, these 17 plants supplied over 10% of the Chinese nations' water requirements. And because this 187 million cubic meters was pristine, this pure water could be used to dilute the effects of the Yellow River to supply the parched farm lands.

A Swedish study suggested that about four million people died needlessly because the old communist government was so opposed to using the new Japanese technology. This lead to the frustration that culminated in the immolation of the Forbidden City.

5

HYPER VIOLENCE IN AMERICA: THE "WOLFIE" PHENOMENON

By Masaru Watanabe
Tokyo University, Department of Psychology
Monday, 25 March 2041

MOST RETROSPECTIVES TODAY LAY THE ROOT of America's epidemic of extreme violence, now more commonly referred to as Hyper Violence or Mob Hyper Violence to the election of the left-leaning mayor of New York City in 2013; a mayor who adopted more and more left-wing positions every time the police or firemen went on strike (events that happened at record levels under his regime).

The preceding 12 years had been a period of unprecedented rebirth of America's then-largest city. Until the election of Michael Bloomberg, New York had been on a declining parabola, occasionally interrupted by a brief period of optimism and the view—however

fleeting—of sunny uplands. But these pleasant inter-
ludes were both brief and increasingly rare.

Overall, the leading city of the Empire State—
like most of America—was living the memories of
past glories—glories of the skyscrapers, which were the
first view of the New World for the tired and huddles
masses as they passed through Ellis Island one hundred
and fifty years earlier; the dreams of limitless potential
in a new world freed from the tedium and shackles and
pettiness of Europe.

●

Looking back now, it's likely that the apogee of Pax
Americana was Tuesday, the 19th of December 1944
at Verdun, when America's genius of impatience was so
vividly shown by the foresight of George Patton, when
he answered Eisenhower about how soon Patton could
start a relief of the always lightly-armed airborne troops
of the U.S. 101 trapped by Gerd von Rundstedt at Bas-
togne—"As soon as you're through with me."

●

But from that brilliance, America had slowly, but
ineluctably declined as a great power—losses in Asian
wars from Vietnam to Pakistan; disasters in Iraq and
Afghanistan; and moral and spiritual decline at home.

Few indices of decline were more telling or more tragic than that of the Negroid Illegitimacy Rate or NIR. (The term for Americans of African descent has gone through a large number of iterations, for a very long time it was "Negro;" then—for a short period of 30 years—it was "Black;" then it changed to "African-American;" then it reverted to "Negros," which was mostly used by young Negroid men; then this permuted to "Noz," which was considered cool, hip and modern for all of six weeks; then it reverted to the rather bland and sinisterly pseudo-scientific "Negroid." Doubtless, this term will retain currency for a decade or two, and then be replaced by yet another term.)

Regardless of the adjective used, the main point was that the rate of the illegitimate births skyrocketed from 15% in 1968 to over 70% in 2012. There were a wide range of causes of this disaster, from the well-meaning but ill-conceived ideas of the disgraced President Lyndon Johnson, who was posthumously convicted of the murder of his predecessor on Elm Street in Dallas in 1963, to the left-wing Liberationists (at the time, called "Feminists")—a branch of a now-banned group of women who promulgated the notion that "husbands were unnecessary," to the media who created the fantasy of "SuperWomen."

Regardless of the causes, the effects were always the same—the creation of generations of lumpenproletariat—a mob of degenerate men who rarely, if ever, worked and who collectively slid into an explosive mixture of drugs, violence and extreme misogyny. Lacking any male leaders of the pack—fathers and uncles—these young men gained their knowledge of the external world through Hollywood and video games.

●

It was this volatile cocktail that created the "wolfie" phenomenon as it is now called. As with most social phenomena, this one fed upon itself—one event on YouTube lead to another. It started with frustrated and unemployable black men punching elderly white ladies in the face to see if they could kill these defenseless old ladies in a single blow. One 16-year-old boy boasted to his fellow inmates that he had killed three white "old bitches" in Brooklyn Heights in a single afternoon in April 2019.

When asked why he did this, his reply was, "It made me feel real good."

As U.S. unemployment slowly but ineluctably climbed to 26% in 2028, after the collapse of China, the isolated wolfie changed to the far more sinister profile of gangs. After the early riots, the height of the wolfie pack attack was in Chicago where over 9,000 people were killed in the four weeks of riots. Drones, armed cars, satellites—a plethora of technical matériel—were of no use. Knowing, indeed watching, what the 50,000-strong rioters were doing was of little use when the defenders consisted of traditional beat cops and terrified National Guardsmen, both outnumbered and ludicrously outgunned by the wolfies.

6

THE ELECTRIC POWER
REVOLUTION: 1990 TO 2040

By Yuuto Saitou
Electric Power Research Council of Japan
Tuesday, 2 April 2041

IN 1900 THE PERCENTAGE OF THE AMERICAN GDP generated by the car industry was zero—the automobile industry was yet to be born. By 1930, the percentage was 11%, the GDP's largest single component.

The same rapid change has occurred in the 50 years from 1990 to 2040 in the generation of electricity. Excluding hydroelectricity, before 1990 less than one-hundredth of one percent of electricity in the developed world was generated by solar power. Today, in 2041, under ten percent is *not* generated by solar power. And the extent of "electric" power had increased 12-fold on a per-capita basis since 1990. This is largely because of the near-universal replacement of dirty hydrocarbons with clean Ultra-HTP, the invention of the Hitachi company in Japan working in conjunction with the AEG company of Germany. Ultra-HTP is now used in everything from passenger stratosphere airliners to 18-wheel trucks in the Greater United States.

●

The development of solar power in this seminal 50-year period is divided into the two sub-histories: traditional and JAXAPower.

Clearly the most important of these technological developments have been the development of the JAXAPower, which in just 15 years has made the use of hydrocarbon fuels obsolete by providing extremely inexpensive electricity throughout the world. And just as aluminum smelters sprang up near sources of cheap and bountiful hydroelectricity in the twentieth century, so the extreme low cost of the electricity generated by JAXAPower provided the impetus to develop Ultra-HTP or Hydrogen Peroxide Power or "HyPower" as it generally called.

The limitless support of electricity that JAXA-Power supplies now means that HyPower has become the new standard for all powered flight. It is true that HyPower does require exceptional engineering—even a 90 degree bend can potentially cause an explosion, or an "Unexpected Combustional Event," in the euphemisms of the HyPower industry. But there are over 100 companies now certified to build and refuel HyPower plants. The net effect is hydrocarbon-based flight is now as dated as the Wright's first flights in North Carolina, with its four-cylinder engine with suction input valves generating all of 12 horsepower.

When the old United States had a monopoly on atomic electricity generation in the early 1950s, many American power utility executives spoke glowingly of "power too plentiful to meter." But this fantasy ended almost in another form of glowing that the executives did not mean—the never-ending disasters of Three Mile Island, Chernobyl, Fukushima Daiichi, and worst of all, the Chicago disaster of 2022 that killed 4,000, after the city defaulted in 2019. To "save money" the city reduced the inspections of the cooling pipes and pumps by 75%; it was three of these pumps that failed at the same time that caused the meltdown (actually one had already failed, but no one had noticed).

With the 167 JAXAPower plants now in operation throughout the world, bountiful and limitless electricity has now become a reality. But this is the development of the past twenty years, from 2021 to 2041.

●

Equally important is the development is the earlier period of 1990 to 2021 where conventional solar power started to displace hydrocarbon and atomic power.

In this earlier period, the two sources were solar cells and wind turbines. Both of these have a colorful history, peppered as it is with an entertaining array of villains and constant double-dealing and back stabbing by governments worldwide as they jockeyed for dominance, and sometimes attempted to kill the infant in the crib (as was the case with the Russian attacks on the United European Power Grid, initially ludicrously described by the Kremlin as attacks by the Arabs).

●

The trio of players in the early stages of solar panel development were the old United States, the former EU, and pre-Confederation China.

In retrospect, it is hard for people today looking back to those earlier years to understand the bizarre—and seemingly irrational—behavior of these three players. In those times the now-discredited concept of "dumping" was still in vogue, and indeed, considered a legitimate economic and legal concept. Fortunately this atavistical misunderstanding was finally laid to rest by the work of the two Chicago economists, Steve Lee and Thomas Benison, for which they received the 2032 Nobel Prize in Economics.

This gist of the work by Lee and Benison is that the concept of dumping was viewed the wrong way— through the wrong end of the telescope as it were. The classical view of dumping was that the perpetrator was attempting to destroy the industrial base of another country by deliberately selling a product or service at a price below cost. According to this notion, once the competitors in the other country had been bank-rupted, the villainous perpetrators were then free to charge whatever they liked as they were now the sole source of the required product or service.

As Lee and Benison point out in their review of the history of dumping, this concept did have some credence and credibility 200 years ago when factories and plants did take years, or even decades, to construct and before the free flow of information via the Zetta Pipes. Governments in the past fifty years have also fol-lowed the same nonsensical approach when they tried to tax multinational corporations.

In both these cases—dumping and taxation—the flawed assumption was that it was difficult, expensive, and tedious to build new factories, or open new offices in new countries.

●

Today, the reality is that an automated solar cell plant can be constructed in six weeks. Both the construction of the factory and actual operation is now done completely by robots. And these robots are themselves built by other robots. In June 2039, Fanuc—the world's leading robotic company—built a solar cell factory in northern Hokkaido in nine days. And this factory was constructed completely by robots controlled from the central Fanuc control center located near Mount Fuji; the control center itself is fully automated. From the loading of the components for the production line from the automated factories in Yokohama onto the automated ships, to the loading of the final output of the solar cells onto the ships to be sent to the customer's destination, no human touched the product. (According to the Robotics Business Review, Fanuc now—in 2041—is larger than the other nine largest robotics companies combined.)

●

The most difficult intellectual aspect of this new approach was the recognition that it was possible at all—a little like the idea of manned flight in 1903. It took years to make the mental leap fully understand the implication and the concepts of RBR—Robots Building Robots. The very earliest stage of RBR was started by the now defunct Google Corporation of the old United States that used mapping cars initially driven by humans and then by robots to map the world's streets. While these cars were quickly superseded by airdrones, the robotic concept had taken hold.

Then it was a small step to move from robots being built by humans in factories to robots being built by robots in factories. Of course, with the replacement of human error, robotic automation provides production output increases that would have made Karl Marx shudder—widespread RBR made all the economic and political theories of the past 200 years completely obsolete.

●

In an amusing piece of theatre at the Fanuc testing grounds, politicians were shown an infinite circle where two robots worked in tandem, one digging a hole in the ground and the second filling it in. The shape traced out was the mathematical sign of infinity—a sideways figure eight. The Fanuc team called this infinite circle, "The Dream of Keynes." One wry part of this theatre was the first robot was programmed to work two percent faster than the second. So inevitably the first robot got ahead of the second. After the first robot got two holes clear of the second robot, the first one would pause, and a computer-generated voice was heard to say, "Don't just stand there, hurry up and get cracking" in the purest Cockney accent; the politicians gasped as they immediately saw the implications—politicians cannot get a robot's vote.

●

As Lee and Benison so brilliantly showed, dumping was counterproductive. The actual effect of this so-called dumping was to provide a subsidy to the buying country. This was most pronounced in the case of solar cells, which are especially easy to make at a robotic factory.

The first countries to take advantage of this inadvertent subsidy were Germany and Switzerland. Even as early as 2013, on some days over 60% of electricity generated in Germany was generated by solar power. By 2023, Germany was generating in excess of 300% of all of Europe's electricity needs. Of course, this lead to significant political change, as countries attempted to maintain a national power generation capacity using discredited nuclear power and antiquated and polluting fossil fuels. But in the face of the overwhelming cost savings—German solar electricity was less than the fifth the cost of old nuclear and fossil electricity—political change was inevitable.

●

It was the Austrian economist Joseph Schumpeter in his 1942 book *Capitalism, Socialism and Democracy* who promulgated the concept of Creative Destruction. This concept, true in the real world, is diabolical to the world's politicians. And just as the Germans and Swiss had so wisely embraced it, other European countries did the opposite. In a move that would have warmed the heart of Ned Ludd, France, Spain, and Italy all passed laws to prevent the use of cheap German and Swiss electricity, "to protect home markets and power utilities." These laws were similar to the ones passed to protect the established gas lighting utilities in the 1880s when the young Edison's direct current electricity first appeared. And they were about as effective.

These contentious laws, more than anything else, lead to the ad hoc formation of the HelveticaReichMark (HRM) currency. Initially it was used just as a virtual currency—an accounting nicety—for the sale of German and Swiss electricity. But as is so often the case with real innovation, it displaced the Euro that was in its death throes.

One of the main beneficiaries of the massive increase of ultra-cheap electricity was the "European" rail network, or more accurately the German-Swiss European Rail Network. In the first phase this new rail network consisted of upgrading existing track and signaling by the European Rail Consortium of Plasser & Theurer, Siemens, and ThyssenKrupp. In a repeat of history, the logo of the consortium was the three interlocking circles of seamless railway tires patented by Alfred Krupp two centuries ago.

At first, this upgrading was limited to Switzerland, Austria, and Germany. But by 2019 the huge economic benefits of the Ultra High Speed trains forced the formerly recalcitrant countries of France, Spain and Italy to come, cap in hand, to request their rail systems be upgraded by the consortium. As part of this first tranche of upgrades, the HelveticaReichMark was mandated as the sole currency of exchange. By 2020, the Euro was dead.

●

As happened in the demise of China, the Euro was not killed—it is still the official currency of 21 European countries. But like European royalty, its purpose has become purely symbolic, just without the smart uniforms and pretty dresses. The national currencies were effectively re-introduced by the simple sleight of hand of national HRMs—there is now an Italian HRM and a Spanish HRM, and a French HRM, and so one. And with the trading of what is called "HRM Pairs" in Zurich and Frankfurt, currency trading was back with a vengeance—Jean-Baptiste's aphorism seemed apropos: *"Plus ça change, plus c'est la même chose."*

So today a housewife buys a melon in Madrid, and the price is listed as 0.65 E-HRM and her shopping card has the amount deducted.

●

The second phase was the development of the two legs of the Direct Current Interconnect. The first leg crossed from Africa to Europe at Gibraltar. The first test cable was laid in 2016 and was an underwater suspension bridge—essentially it was simply a wire cable at a depth of 300 meters. As the German engineers had predicted, sure enough a Panama-registered oil tanker inadvertently dragging its anchor chain snagged and destroyed the test cable.

Smugly, the German engineers got their way and the actual power conduit was buried on the seafloor. Actually, "buried" is the wrong word—the cable was laid on the sea floor on a carbon fiber matting and was then covered with a tapered concrete sheath to a depth of four meters. Tests with all the common ship anchors in use proved the effectiveness of this design.

The actual interconnect is 1.5 meters in diameter and consists of the copper core that is cryogenically chilled by liquid nitrogen to reduce internal resistance to almost zero; pumping stations at each end re-cool the nitrogen. Over 70 terawatts pass through this "cable" from the 121 generating stations in Morocco and Tunisia.

The second leg, completed in 2034, was at the other end of the Mediterranean.

●

Even with the first Interconnect, the energy profile and personality of Europe was radically altered. For the first time households, industry and the rapidly expanding rail network got energy at undreamed of prices—the price of electricity for all households dropped from 60 of the old Euros per megawatt in 2011 to 0.1 old Euros in 2027 (or 50 HRM to 0.09 HRM).

This revolution made the traditional electric utilities as relevant as gas lighting companies at the start of the 1900s. Virtually none of the established power companies with their inefficient and polluting coal plants and their even more sinister and odious nuclear stations survived. Having all taken the ostrich-in-the-sand approach they had simply lobbied harder and harder with their political supporters for more and more laws to halt progress. And all to no avail. It was true that the French were most vociferous in the defense of this Ancien Régime, but like the earlier Kingdom of France, this defense was pointless; think 1870 and Krupp and France's defeat, or 1940 and the Wehrmacht and France's defeat, or 1954 and Giap and France's defeat; the French being the world's champions at losing wars.

●

While households and industry were the two most obvious beneficiaries of the 500-fold decrease in electricity costs in the four decades from 2014, it was actually the rail system that gained the greatest advantage. And this advantage came about in two different ways. The first was the re-engineering of existing diesel locomotives' motive power with the new HyPower engines, where the HPP was generated by electricity; the second was the spread of electrification. In the first case, the Hydrogen Peroxide engines were a simple refit that typically took under four days (this was reduced to six hours in 2025 with the robotic replacement plants.) The second was the construction of the universal power feeds that are now a common sight on all of Europe's main lines.

•

Another significant effect of the new electricity was the closing of the Russian natural gas pipelines. The earliest of these pipelines dated from 1982. From the start, the dependency on Russian natural gas provide to be highly contentious and as Russia lurched from one political crisis to another, so the critics grew and became more vocal.

The development of energy independence, led by Germany, removed the need for Russian natural gas. Ending the use of Russian natural gas, coupled with the creating of the new rail links to the Ukraine meant that Russia became first isolated, and then irritated, and then dismayed. The final step was the street battles.

•

Not a few German politicians of the period were convinced that the Russian pipelines were like opium pipes in Victorian London. Just as the earlier generations of school boys recoiled in horror as that most Victorian of fictional characters suffered the poisonous fumes of Upper Swindon Lane, so German politicians saw the smiling Russian face as even more wicked and horrible. The Germans fear—reasonable, as it happened—was that the Russians had never forgotten the horrific battles of Slavs and Germans 75 years earlier. And while the regimes had changed, and the hatred had notionally ended, in reality nothing had changed—it was Lebensraum redux.

The wiser of the German politicians had been preaching this since the opening of the first pipeline. After the solar revolution, all German politicians adopted it. It took only twenty years after the introduction of the HRM for Germany to buy most of Russian territory where the Wehrmacht had bled to death; Lebensraum redux indeed.

7

INTELLECTUAL DECLINE AND THE NATION STATE: 2022 TO 2041

By Peter Clarke
London Institute Of Advanced Studies
Friday, 26 April 2041

EVEN AS RECENTLY AS FORTY YEARS AGO, it was considered *de rigueur* that north Asia countries were "backward" in the position of women in society—having women staying at home nurturing their children was considered by all in the West as antiquated and atavistical dogma from a bygone age.

This was in spite of the abundance of evidence of the pernicious effects of illegitimacy. By 2018, 92% of all black births in the old United States were born out of wedlock and the overall U.S. rate had exceeded 50%. Numerous academic studies had already proven that illegitimacy leads to the child having a five time greater rate of being in prison, a three-fold greater chance of suicide and, perhaps most troubling of all, a four times greater rate of drug addiction.

In contrast the illegitimacy rate in Japan today in 2041 is 1.3%.

One simply has to spend an hour or two at the small playground next to the Imperial Palace in Tokyo to see the beneficial effects of attentive mothers. Clustered in small groups, these mothers entertain and encourage their children who are—naturally enough— all well-adjusted and content. These mothers arrive on their electric bicycles with one or two children, often chatting with their offspring.

The OECD intelligence tests are an objective measure of the efficacy of this type of child-rearing: the average IQ of an eight-year old Japanese child is over 16 points higher than a similar child in the U.S. This is often considered one reason Japanese never loot. For example, in the Los Angeles earthquake of 2026, over six percent of the adult males were arrested or detained for looting or suspicion of looting when the National Guard was finally called in; in the Osaka earthquake of 2037, three males were arrested (or 0.00067% of the population.)

●

Another useful metric of the wisdom of traditional Japanese child rearing is the overall change in per capita income in the Robotic Age—while U.S. per capita income has plummeted in the past forty years, the average per capita income in Japan has had a steady year-over-year increase of almost three percent. Apples to apples.

●

What investors want are countries with a high intellectual property density—countries with the best technical universities and universities, moreover, that work closely with industry. In reality, there were very few countries that meet even this simple criterion.

In the West, universities have slowly inched back to a time five hundred years earlier—they appeared modern with all the latest technical gadgets and energy saving devices, but they had lost the only trait a university actually needed, that of open enquiry. The new dark ages has cast its ugly shadow over the universities in many countries; it was as if the Spanish Inquisition had been reborn but with the advantage this time of worldwide communications at the speed of light.

In one notable case, an academic had openly pondered if there might be some kind of DNA link between women and their lack of interest in the hard sciences. In other words, the type of reasonable and open questioning that could occur in any tutorial or a Common Room over a glass of claret.

What actually happened would have made a Dominican monk smile—out with the Wheel, the Rack, and of course, out with the quill and paper for the confession. Instead of showing the weakness of the conjecture, the victim was violently and viciously attacked *ad hominem*. Essentially he was a modern day Galileo without even the chance to whisper, "but it does move."

A similar case was that of an historian of economics who had made the most horrible transgression to wonder if a homosexual, indeed a pedophile, economist's quip of "*In the final analysis, we're all dead*" may not have been partially the result of him not having had children.

If the naïve academic pondering DNA was bad enough, this second case struck at the very bedrock of modern dogma; it would be like stating that Mary, of rosary fame, was a lesbian. (Not that, of course, there would be anything wrong with that. No, no, no—not at all. This is not to imply, or even suggest that Mary couldn't have been so. Why, Mary had the right to choose her own sexual preference...)

The modern Inquisition share a great deal in common with the one in Spain: refusal to testify is a sign of guilt; anyone and everyone is free to testify against him; and witnesses on his behalf are ignored.

These cases are most prevalent in the countries that formerly were open and encouraged different views. The leading examples are the United States (where the above two heretics live), the United Kingdom and France.

●

Watching from afar with a sense of wry bemusement, the universities of German-speaking Europe, Greater Israel, Formosa, and Japan moved forward to the 22nd century, while the fiscally weakening countries turned in on themselves—as is always the case—and reopened the debate on the number of angels that could fit on the head of a pin; actually it was the number of mandatory courses in "Transsexual Diversity And The Human Experience" that should be required to graduate. (One antediluvian curmudgeon foolishly muttered, "In my day, it was English." The utterance, overheard by the head of the Equality and Fairness Supervisor, was sufficient for the Board to recommend early retirement, with—of course—a reduced pension.)

8

THE BIRTH AND DEATH OF THE EURO

By Stephan Kurtz
Nobel Foundation of North German
Monday, 29 April 2041

IT IS OFTEN SAID THAT POLITICAL DISCOURSE is really only the entertainment for the chattering classes; then—in a surprisingly short period—the truth becomes clear.

A good example is the idea of communism. First embraced in practical earnest in 1917, by 1992 it was seen to be a fraud, albeit by then over 250 million people had perished because of it. Chic and fashionable as it was among the English proponents of "The Higher Sodomy," and then by the Cambridge-based clique who detested seeing their Empire destroyed by a loud, vulgar, and unsophisticated America. And there was no shortage of high government officials on the other side of the Atlantic who saw it as their own personal salvation and meaning-in-life.

Generally, within a lifetime, an idea can be proven true or false. And it is often less than a lifetime. Such is the case of the bizarre notion of the single European currency, called the "Euro."

Briefly, the Euro came into existence—rather romantically—on 1 January 1999, and was effectively replaced by the HRM twenty years later.

The reason for the existence of the Euro was to attack the United States. Of course, this was never stated, or even alluded to, but all the same the rationale was clear from the outset: how could a disparate collection of little nation states compete with the might of the United States, especially as all these European nation states were constantly bickering among themselves like a typically drunk Irish family on a summer Saturday night in Dublin? No. That would not do, or so the Eurocrats reasoned. However, the basic problem of these cerebral but terribly impractical academics was that they had never run a business. So—like a celibate priest teaching sex to a nervous engaged couple—it was the blind leading the blind.

●

The Morgenthau Plan was conceived by Henry Morgenthau in 1944 to destroy Germany by destroying all its industry and replacing the factories with farms. The concept, immediately embraced by Stalin, was to push Germany back 500 years by razing Germany's industry.

The paradox was the Euro did precisely this, not to Germany, but to the so-called victors of the second phase of the Great European Civil War—while Greater Germany got stronger and stronger in the 20 years after the introduction of the ill-conceived Euro, France, Italy, Spain, et al., become weaker and weaker. The same could be said for England (then still called the United Kingdom).

●

The first ten years after the adoption of the HRM, Europe more or less stabilized. But the Great Riot of 2029 in Paris radically changed this. The Great Riot is described elsewhere in this publication, but suffice to say, when the Louvre was ravaged by the mobs, the world, and in particular German-speaking Europe was outraged.

Central European Security Forces (CESF), led by the Swiss, were at the Louvre within two hours. Using their new disabling tear gas, the CESF police were able to secure the museum in 15 minutes. Outside, the Paris police were less than pleased. It was only the appearance of the French President, Ms. Marine Le Pen and the hordes of HyperVision channels that calmed the situation.

In what was likely the shortest surrender ceremony of any nation ever, Ms. Le Pen asked the CESF to work with the Louvre staff to secure both the building and the art. Le Pen is reputed to have said, "*Here are my Switzers, let them guard the door* [sic]." In an aside, never seen even by the HV operators, Le Pen requested all the art be moved to Berlin for safe keeping.

9

THE PARADOX OF GROWTH: JAPAN 2014 TO 2041

By Haruto Ishii
The Tokyo Centre For The Study Of East Asia
Wednesday, 1 May 2041

FIFTY YEARS AGO, MUCH WAS MADE of the seemingly unsustainable debt of Japan—predictions of catastrophe and worse were all over the traditional media of press, television, and the old Internet. Instead, the opposite happened: along with Greater Israel (which in 2038, incorporated the old Saudi Arabia), Germany and Formosa, Japan's past 50 years have been one of stable and consistent growth. Also, the dire population bomb never exploded—the aging population has been an inadvertent asset to Japan.

So how has this occurred and what were the driving forces that made this possible? This article will touch on some of the more important causes of this unexpected development.

Probably the most significant factors determining Japan's renaissance were external to Japan: the collapse of the so-called Expatriated Nation States (ENS) where excessively large populations that exacerbated large fissures and schisms in the social, racial, and economic classes. The two prime examples most often quoted are the Greater United States and India. Even as early as 2025, it was clear the old United States was on a steeply declining hyperbola, and this decline and decay only accelerated after the disastrous merging of the old state of Mexico with the former 48 mainland states of the old United States. In the opinion of many, this was one of the primary causes of the desultory four-way civil war that has raged on and off in Greater America for over ten years.

Canada, protected as it is with its massive 90-foot triple walls that run the entire length of its border with its southern neighbor looks more like Europe during the 100-Year War, but this is described in detail by others.

Just like the Greater United States, the old desiccated nation state of India suffered a similar fate, but for very different reasons. Whereas in the Greater United States, the internal strife was based on race, in what was then India, it was based on religion. Both countries shared the dubious distinction of suffering the disaster of massive corruption; corruption had always been a problem in India since the British—whose bankruptcy after the First World War was exacerbated after the end of the Second—gave up trying to rule India in 1947.

In the old United States, corruption had been fairly mild until the bizarre merging with Mexico. In fact, the Clinton Presidency of 2020 to 2023 was reputed to be one of the cleanest in the history of the Republic. After her sudden and tragic death from breast cancer, all this changed. Then came the integration of Mexico and first the infection, and then the destruction, of the old Anglo tradition by the universally corrupt practices of the hispanophones—President Sebastián López made Ulysses Grant look like an angel. The list of transgressions of López is too long and too ugly to list here, and it is covered in detail elsewhere in this publication.

●

The cornerstone of the British rule of India was the universality of English. The ubiquity of English in one stroke dampened the massive amount of religious discord, and indeed open hatred, in the subcontinent. But after the British left, more and more of these previously quiescent factions gained confidence. With that confidence came stridency. The renaming of Bombay to Mumbai was an early manifestation of this return to barbarism, which the British had so successfully eradicated.

●

The spark that started the Indian Mutiny of 1857 was the spreading of the false rumor that the paper cartridges of the new Enfield rifles were greased with animal fat, namely beef and pork. This effectively offended both the Hindus with their reverence of cows, and the Mohammedans with the abhorrence of pork. The main point here is that India—more than any country in the world—lived (and clearly died) by religion. India lacked the 4,000 year history of Japan, and India also lacked a Martin Luther; cults, and deities, no matter how bizarre and unhealthy, were not only tolerated in India, but encouraged. And this unique fanaticism was the cause of the fatal destruction of the old country of India.

●

A number of articles and books over the past decade have shown that nations with populations over 100 million are inherently unstable and inevitably self-destruct. Until as recently as the start of the current century, it was taken as infallible dogma that larger nations had unique benefits over smaller ones. This was largely based on the ideas of economies of scale, where larger nations could muster and organize and arrange a large and coherent work force. And at that time, and in earlier times, that may very well have been true.

●

But the advent of Total Robotic Construction (TRC), created and refined by Germany, Greater Israel, and Japan, most factories are now empty of people. As just one simple example consider the Toyota/Mercedes factory in Yokosuka. The location was the old U.S. Navy base that had been dormant since the controversial departure of the Americans from Japanese soil back in 2020. This factory is staffed by four people. The key to this factory's success was the new design concepts developed in the 2020s and 2030s where components were designed around the then-new idea of automation.

In the past, every article about cars was accompanied by the prerequisite photograph of an assembly line, with human workers hovering around partially built cars, like worker bees around their queen. Twenty years ago all this changed with the introduction of the Japan Robotic Engineering Standards or JRES for short. These standards stood car construction on its head.

In the early 1920s Henry Ford revolutionized car construction with the invention of the assembly line, and an idea he pinched from the meat processing plants that dotted Chicago at that time, but with the new JRES guidelines, components were designed with one and just one goal in mind—to be easy for a robot to handle the component.

For example, since the earliest cars, generators and then alternators were driven off fan belts. It is true the technology of the belts themselves changed over time, from the humble V belt to the toothed belt to the Kevlar belt. But the basic idea had not changed for 150 years, derived as it was from the power shafts that distributed power through British factories at the start of the first Industrial Revolution.

With the introduction of JRES, all alternators were driven off the central gear train, and were held in a cast and machined cavity off to the side of the central gear train. The purpose of this radical change from the old belt drive was to enable the robot's claws to easily add the alternator.

The alternator itself was assembled in a TRC factory in Hokkaido and shipped by the new AutoRail system to the central assembly plant in Yokosuka. By adopting these TRC concepts, factories can now run 24 hours a day, 365 days a year, and by having the standard Japanese approach of two production lines and one maintenance line, production is now always consistent. (The maintenance line is used when one of the other two lines are halted for maintenance and refurbishing. With the advanced refurbishing standards now used, no unscheduled downtime or failures are ever encountered.)

The real benefits of TRC are obvious: inconsistent, unreliable, and tardy human employees are a thing of the past; the idea of withdrawal of labor—what used be describe by the archaic terms of "strike" and "Work To Rule"—are now long lost dreams of now disbanded "unions." (A union was a group of workers who banded together to blackmail and to coerce employers. Some unions were based on employer—the now default American car makers located in Detroit were one example. Other types of these unions were based on trade—all buggy whip leather workers, or electricians, or railroad workers, or teamsters—men who drove teams of horses.)

Another benefit of TRC is the complete removal of errors—in the old factories and plants almost all the errors were due to human error—or sabotage—not machine failure. So, with the removal of the old humans-based assembly lines, errors were removed as well. This is much the same as airlines today where the pilots—always prone to selfish suicides—have been replaced by computers.

One interesting element that was not re-discovered until TRC became universal was the great importance of temperature and humidity—with hot, and sweaty workers, the ambient climate controls in the old factories was very hit-and-miss. It was the Japanese, along with their German colleagues, who found that even the earliest TRC factories were producing products that were astonishing in their consistency and quality. This massive difference with the old human plants—the difference was often in excess of 100,000 to one—was found to be caused by the humans' sweating and breathing. (The Japanese had actually reviewed their records from the 1930s and 1940s from ball bearing factories; the limits of tolerance in these old-style factories were determined solely by the quality of the air conditioning, in those days called "manufactured air.")

This discovery led to first the Japanese, and then the Germans, in building the first hermetically-sealed nitrogen factories. With these factories there was no moisture, and the temperature was controlled to within one-hundredth of a degree. With these second-generation TRC factories, tolerances previously undreamed of were made possible on production lines for cars. This was actually one of the main driving forces for the creation of LeatherX, the patented product of the Swiss-Japanese Nippon-Helvetica company. This new material is identical to cow leather in all respects apart from it being not being organic. LeatherX has the same exact texture and consistency of animal hides, but just no moisture. Using the words of the world of fashion, it has the same "feel," as blind "taste tests" proved.

All input and output from TRC factories is via "air locks" that are actually four separate locks of nitrogen. It is actually a three phase operation: first a partial vacuum is created to remove all the moisture-laden air, then dry and hot nitrogen is pumped in to a pressure of three atmospheres, then this second wash is removed and replaced with the final TRC nitrogen; the entire process takes four seconds.

●

At the end of last century, dire warnings started surfacing about Japan's declining birthrate—one of the earliest white papers was written by a trio of researchers from the bastion of the extreme Left, Harvard University in 1992.

The gist of all these white papers and warnings were the same: from 2000 to 2060 Japan's population would be reduced by one-third, and moreover, the ratio of workers to retirees would balloon from 2:1 to 1:3—a six-fold change. A small army of Cassandras screeched that a huge program would be needed immediately to import maids and caregivers from the Philippines and Indonesia to care for the rapidly increasing population of Japanese retirees. In addition academics and politicians collectively wrung their hands about how these caregivers would be paid for, as they were not actually producing anything.

Much like the U.S. federal government's research project to build a superior iron lung for advanced cases of polio, these fears were completely and entirely ephemeral. As was the case of the unimaginative bureaucrats, technology and innovation trumped governmental plodding.

The invention of the Salk vaccine made iron lungs unnecessary. In precisely the same manner, just under 100 years later, the invention of Differential Microdiagnosis by the researchers at the Hitachi Research Laboratories in Tokyo made the need to import even a single Filipina equally unnecessary.

The heart of this new invention was five microdiagnosis implants, one in ends of each of the four extremities, and a slightly larger one in the upper left gluteus muscle. These five implants all sent radio signals to the local computer located in the retiree's home and this data was then transmitted to the central computer center in Tokyo.

What the inventors at Hitachi had discovered—and what they received the 2027 Nobel Prize in Medicine for—was that it was the rate of change of the differences in the reading that was the key to monitoring a mammal's health. (The invention was very quickly adopted by farmers in Japan to improve the health of livestock.)

By having micro-implants in the toes and thumbs, the technology was able to record five metrics. Somewhat surprisingly, the most useful was the simplest, namely temperature. Actually it was the rate of change of the differences in temperature that was the critical factor. In the first year of widespread implementation, strokes had been reduced by 78%, and the concomitant hospital treatments were reduced by the same amount. The financial savings—not to mention the reduction in human suffering—were astronomical.

As is generally the case with new technologies these days, the real breakthrough was in the software not the microdiagnosis implants; "nano technology" had been around for close to 50 years in one form or another, and it was simply a matter of time to wait for the Haldane's Curve to be reached. (The Haldane's Curve is the conjecture, named after Professor Haldane of Cambridge University, that held that the size of microdiagnosis implants would halve every 18 months—this conjecture is often misquoted as every two years, but the actual paper in the "Institute of Nano Technology" published on the 19th of April 2017 stated every 18 months.)

As it soon discovered, a stroke is not a sudden *unpredictable* event. It may have seemed so 100 years ago, but now the dynamics—almost the personality— of a stroke are now completely understood and strokes have been classed into five distinct classes by JISO. It was found that the temperature differentials of a stroke start around 36 hours before the actual catastrophic event. By doing extensive analysis by the Hitachi proprietary algorithms, the first of the three stages of a stroke could be easily detected and a nurse dispatched to the patient's home.

With the spectacular success of the Hitachi invention, patients around the world were immediately queuing to get this 'miracle' technology for themselves. The Hitachi company was happy to license the microdiagnosis probes and hardware to 17 countries in the first two years of commercial release of the service, but the heart of the service—the software running on the Hitachi supercomputers in Tokyo, was never licensed. All the data was piped across to Tokyo; this continues to this day. Actually "Tokyo" is somewhat of a misleading abbreviation as the Hitachi company established what used to be called "Super Cloud Data Centers" in nine Japanese cities.

With the Zetta Pipes installed at no cost by the WCP, Hitachi estimates that health of all of the world's human and animal population can be easily monitored.

●

Another of the three arrows of growth for Japan in the past 50 years has been the growth of Foreign Direct Investment or FDI. This grown has mostly happened since 2027, the year of the massive American Default and the Chinese Massacres (other papers in this Yearbook describe these momentous events).

"Fair, Clean, And Healthy" was the rather puerile FDI slogan of the old Ministry of Economy, Trade and Industry (METI). However unimaginative and bureaucratic, the slogan did summarize why outside investors flooded to Japan after the events of 2027.

To better understand the sudden upswing in FDI in Japan, it is necessary to look no further than the old United States (before its anschluss with Mexico). In

2000, the old U.S. got 37% of the world's FDI, but by 2012 that share had dwindled to 17%, and after 2021 and the promulgation of the dire "Protection Of The Dollar" laws by a frightened Congress, the percentage had collapsed to under 2%; by 2023, Vietnam—with a population of less than one third of the old U.S.—was getting almost twice as much FDI as the U.S.

Investors around the world, who had traditionally—and without thinking—invested in North America now voted with their feet and their money. However the world had become increasingly unstable with both political uncertainty as well as radical new technologies destroying old investment aphorisms.

The old, quaint and now discredited "BRIC" quartet of Brazil, Russia, China, and India had a mild popularity for about ten years at the turn of the century. But like most guff from most investment banks in most countries in most years, this one proved to be close to worthless. What investors wanted was a stable country, one that had growth potential and an avoidance of primary producers. The last point—big holes in the ground—ruled out Russia, Canada, and Australia. These countries essentially produced nothing, they simply dug things up and exported the raw material to Europe or China. And as such had massive economic swings—the classic boom and bust.

10

THE DESIGN CONCEPTS OF THE F89 HYPER FIGHTER

By Dr. Joseph Issacs
Dean of Aeronautics, Tel Aviv Technical University
Thursday, 9 May 2041

UNTIL LAST WEEK, THE DESIGN OF THE F89 HF had been classed as an UltraSecret. As such, the details of the design were limited to the executive of the four nations of the World Council for Peace (WCP) of Japan, Germany, Greater Israel, and the Commonwealth of Formosa.

With the unanimous vote by the WCP Executive to de-classify the details of the F89, I have been requested to provide a general lay description of the history of the F89 design.

I am happy to do so. Much has been made in the world press of my involvement in the creation of the F89. And I should like to take this opportunity to explain that while it is true I was the lead designer, a project of this magnitude and of this audacity is not the work of one man or even one team. All complex designs these days is always an effort of a large group of specialists—no one man designs a product as complex and as innovative as the F89. To suggest I was "ably assisted" is completely and entirely misleading—I was little more than the ring master of a very talented international circus. It is true that I did a lot of the original design of the hyper engines (ably assisted by my team at TATU), that is the start and the end of my creative involvement in this invention. The hyper engines, while new and novel, were just one small part of this project. Over 94% of the design was done by others—the software was developed by the Japanese Advanced Project Institute in Tokyo; the telematics by the Deutsche Technical University in Munich and ETH in Zurich; the aerodynamics was the work of the Formosa Technical University in Taipei; and the integration with the Japanese/German Location Facility (JGLF) was performed by the Japanese and German Software Design Company (JGSC). In short, no one person, indeed, no one country in the WCP, can be credited with the development of the F89.

The design team I assembled in 2035 was provided with the rare opportunity in technology of starting with a clean sheet of paper—a complete blank canvas. Most weapons systems in the past were simply a refinement of existing technologies. As an example, think of the development of the first Dreadnoughts at the start of the last century—these were ships that were simply larger, faster, and more heavily armed than their predecessors, but the same overall technology—large armored ships with big guns—the fabled All Big Guns ship. In contrast, we were in the same position as when the Merrimack destroyed the wooden Union ships at Hampton Roads on Saturday, 8 March 1862—all existing designs were suddenly obsolete.

●

A more recent—and certainly more germane case—was the encounter of the first flight of eight F89s when they annihilated the remnants of the old Royal Saudi Air Force of 108 antiquated F35 fighters, which the Saudis had purchased from the Greater United States thirty year earlier; all 108 F35s were destroyed in seventeen minutes. This, in no small part, leads to the destruction of the old Saudi empire, and its integration into Greater Israel.

But, I am getting ahead of myself.

When I was first given the task of designing the F89, I asked myself one simple question: how can today's modern technology best be used to create effective air supremacy? As I have mentioned, it is a fatal mistake to simply improve an existing technology. What is needed is a new way of thinking based on the developments in technology in the past thirty years.

So with these changes in mind, I sat down to create a design document using modern technology.

So what does this mean in practice?

The new JGLF, which provides geographic location to within one millimeter compared to 15,000 millimeters of the old U.S. GPS system, and with a reliability undreamed of by the old U.S.-based system that was often unreliable and worse exposed to the political machinations of the old U.S. military (most people living today can still recall the mayhem caused by the unilateral shutdown of the old GPS system for three weeks in 2027).

One of the most important ramifications is that the idea of a blue-sea navy of a massive and ponderous aircraft carrier group and its multiplicity of support vessels—destroyers, cruisers, and support vessels—was as relevant in today's world as wooden hulled ships in Hampton Roads on the Ninth of March 1862.

●

The old U.S. Navy's love of aircraft carrier groups—such as the old Seventh Fleet—proved to be totally irrelevant. These aircraft carriers—little changed since the Battle of Midway—were based on the now-discredited notion of throwing manned aircraft into the air to attack a target, and then to return to the mother carrier at the end of the mission. And these aircraft would be heavy and controlled by the human pilots, with assistance from the mother carrier's intelligence. This approach had many weaknesses, such as requirement of aircraft carriers of massive size, with steam-powered catapults and very long flight decks. The very size of these behemoths meant a top speed of 30 knots at best (and even at these modest speeds many of the support vessels were unable to keep up).

So this was one of my main starting points: because the F89 is less than one-tenth the weight of the old F35, far more aircraft could be carried on board; as the F89 is powered by the HyPower with a five-times advantage over crude aviation kerosene used by the F35, no longer were ponderous 'flight decks required; as the F89 was pilotless, the new fighters are be launched more like the old missiles of the 1970s—G-forces were no longer a limitation. Most importantly of all, the F89 is designed—from the ground up—to be launched from high-speed hydrofoils capable of well over 70 knots. And with the unique retrieval system designed by my colleagues at ETH, an F89 can be retrieved by any of a wide group of the new hydrofoil fleet. If one is sunk or disabled, the F89 can be retrieved by another in the group. My study of the end of the Battle of Midway was useful—on the night of Friday 5 June 1942, Spruce decided to fully illuminate TF-16 so his Dauntlesses could land, in spite of many of the pilots not being qualified for night landings. I could see the huge benefits of making the F89, in essence, a super drone, capable of being launched like a missile and of being retrieved like a baseball catcher catching the pitcher's throw.

Of course, an essential part of this was software—the F89 is simply an automated machine that delivers a result, it is no longer a concept of an "aircraft" in the long tradition stretching back to the Red Baron and his ilk over Flanders.

●

Probably the best proof of this concept was the sorties launched on the Wednesday and Thursday in May

2040 when the old Saudi Arabia launched the attacks on Tel Aviv and Jerusalem. As the price of oil had plummeted with the rapid adoption of JAXAPower though out most of the world, support for the rulers of that always-brittle theocracy had crumbled. As is often the case in these situations, the rulers fabricated a reason to attack Israel to deflect internal dissent, in much the same manner as the Chinese Communists ceaselessly castigated Japan in spite of their sins being a hundred times worse.

The Greater Israel Defence Agency was alerted to these attacks by the joint WCP Air Command. In a matter of seven minutes, eight of the F89A fighters had been automatically launched from two of the German WCP hydrofoils sitting in the eastern Mediterranean— the *Albert Speer* and the *Angela Merkel.*

With a speed over triple that of the aging F35, and able to support a turn of up to 32G, the F89A made contact with the Saudi planes in 13 minutes. The high G forces were able to be handled by the F89A largely because the F89A had no armor—there was no pilot to protect and the odious and heavy accoutrements of ejector seats, etc., were obviously not needed. Each F89A carried 18 of the new MARS light-weight rockets. With the F89A's unprecedented maneuverability, it was child's play for an F89A to approach the F35 from behind and to drill one of the rockets directly into the gap just above the engine exhaust; result: disintegration.

The F89A would then pull a high-G turn human pilots could only dream of to avoid the detritus of the exploding F35. The F89A fired 108 Mars rockets that day; not one was wasted. Afterwards the rather ostentatious commander had two of the F89As fly to Mecca and had them fly within three centimeters of each of the minarets of the Grand Mosque. At Mach 2, the towers were fatally weakened. At first the pilgrims on the ground thought it was divine providence. Two minute later when all the towers collapsed they were not so sure; when the survivors struggled back to their hotel rooms and saw on the television a broadcast telling them of the defeat at the hands of the WCP, led by the hated Israelis, they then saw it was God's punishment. Two days later the so-called royal family of Saudi Arabia fled to the Dolder Hotel in Zurich, ironically on private flights supplied by JAL; a week later the Swiss froze all of the assets of the House of Saud. The month after that, the former Saudi Arabia—in the Hydrocarbon Era envied throughout the world—meekly became a protectorate in Greater Israel.

11

THE DOMINANCE OF 'ONE VOICE' IN EUROPE, 2010 TO 2041

By Edward Joneson
The New Financial Times, London
Saturday, 11 May 2041

AS WITH THE START OF THE FIRST WORLD WAR, the start of the rise to dominance of the right-wing "One Voice" parties started with a single event. In the case of the trans-national One Voice it was the firebombing of the two buses carrying 134 Swedish policemen by the black migrants in the Stockholm suburb of Husby in July 2021. The police were trying to restore order after seven days of rioting and looting, which had left 17 people dead and over 200 injured.

That summer was one of the hottest on record in northern Europe, and the Swedish rioters had been provided with exceptional role models by the rioters in Paris and Amsterdam. In the French case, it was exclusively black French from Africa, while in the Dutch case it was a curious amalgam of black and Mohammedan rioters. Both ERVs (Extended Riot with Violence) occurred within five days of each other in late June.

What made the Swedish case so appalling was the grisly and calculated way it was carried out. The rioters had stolen delivery vans from the local Amazon depot and had used these vehicles to sandwich in the two police busses. With the two busses next to each other, and the two vans at each end, the rioters simply rocked the buses over. With the two busses now on their sides, it was a simple job for half a dozen men armed with sledge hammers to simply smash the windows of the busses. Then 500 liters of petrol was dumped into each bus followed by a single Molotov.

A television helicopter hovering overhead recorded the images as well as the screams of the policemen being burnt alive.

The most infamous moment came when a second television crew on the ground, through a very nervous interpreter, asked one of the rioters (still proudly holding his stolen sledgehammer) what it was like.

He smiled, showing a row of perfectly white teeth outlined against his carbon-black skin. He paused for effect, still smiling.

"Well, mon, I never realized how much work it was to toast Whitey—I am sweating like a pig."

The interviewer looked at the sound recordist with a look combining horror, disgust, and a great deal of fear—would the four Swedes of the television crew be next?

With a gall that in retrospect seemed bordering on the insane, the interviewer asked the interpreter to ask the man's name.

"Abdikarim Hoodoa, that's my name. In my country it means lucky servant of Mohammad."

Looking at the screen, he smiled that glorious, generous and friendly smile, so at odds with the man.

"You coppers come and get me any time," he said, looking at the camera's lens with amusement like a cat toying with a dying mouse.

While the crew feared for their lives, Mr. Hoodoa simply sauntered off to get his afternoon spliff of ganja.

The feed had been live—direct back to the studio. In the control panel the formerly-proud Swedish producers watched in horror. One woman at the back of the room was quietly sobbing. The lead producer took the unprecedented action of cutting into the regular programming to run this feed as well as the helicopter crew's images and sounds.

•

A television crew had been sent to the home of Björn Johansson, the leader of the Swedish One Voice party. Since its formation in 2017, ironically after an earlier batch of riots in Husby, the party had slowly increased its vote from seven percent to a quite reasonable 19 percent.

The interviewer knocked on the door and it was opened by Mr. Johansson. He looked extremely concerned.

"Please come in. We are watching the broadcasts."

With that, the three people in the crew entered the house and made their way to the first room on the left. On the wall unit were the images. The pixel projection was life-sized so the massive black man with the sledge-hammer was life-size and exceptionally intimidating.

"Please turn that off," the politician said to his wife.

"Pour these people some coffee, please."

"Can you imagine the horror of being burned alive?" he asked the interviewer.

He shook his head.

"I cannot. I cannot believe these images and terrible sounds. This is Sweden. It is 2021. This is not the Dark Ages. My question to you three, as Swedes and just as much as human beings, is how can we have let this develop? My friends on the Left in the parliament accuse me of being stuck in the past, of being unrealistic. But is this the future—'Mon, I never realized how much work it was to toast Whitey—I am sweating like a pig.' Is this what our poor Sweden has sunk to?"

No one in the room spoke for a very, very long time.

Then the bearded young image operator spoke.

"Mr. Johansson I have always believed in equality. While at university I dated a black girl. When we went to her home, her brother and his friends would pay particular attention to me, and in a very unfriendly way. They were clearly extremely concerned that their little sister was being—as they put—'violated by the white man'. Now, none of these fellows had a job, none went to school, none read. All they did was gamble and smoke weed. I always felt a little uneasy, but dismissed it. Today I have seen that I was wrong to dismiss it, it was not just a mild annoyance, but a real and deep hatred. It's madness, isn't it? These people come to Sweden then behave like this. I have never voted for you, and frankly I never dreamt I would, but today has changed me."

The politician nodded and clasped his hands together in front of his face like a minister on Sunday in the pulpit.

"Well, voting for me is not important, I am just one politician. What is important is voting for Sweden. I have often been shouted down for suggesting that we Swedes are naïve and too trusting. Sadly, I think Mr. Hoodoa has proved me correct, even though I would be completely happy to be wrong."

"So what will you do?"

Saying nothing, he removed his phone and clicked two buttons.

"Sorry for disturbing you, Prime Minister, it's Johansson. I think we need to have an all-party meeting this evening."

A long pause as Johansson listened.

"No, I do not think I am overreacting. I think it is our duty."

More listening, this time accompanied by furrowing of the brow.

"OK, well you are the leader of the country."

The three television people were thrilled to have witnessed a fragment of realpolitik.

"The Prime Minister told me that she thought no action was needed."

The imagist shouted, "No action? What in God's name did she mean?"

"Gentlemen, start your equipment, let's change Sweden for the better, right now, right here."

Five minutes later the recording started, and as with the previous broadcasts it was fed directly back to the central control room.

Looking directly into the lens the leader of One Voice started.

"My name is Björn Johansson, and I am the leader of the One Voice party. My party and other political parties like us, both in Sweden and abroad, have been emphasizing the extreme danger and the inevitable disaster of accepting so many migrants. While a few of these people are honest and hardworking, unfortunately many—far too many simply come to Sweden to soak up our social programs and cause strife. And I think the honest and hardworking are an ever-shrinking minority. We have all just seen how Mr. Hoodoa is a perfect example of this second class. What I propose is that all these so-called refugees pass tests in Swedish and have skills to earn a living. Migrants currently in Sweden who fail these two tests will be deported to their country of origin with Swedish passports that expire in seven days. I urge all parties to consider this, and I urge all of you to vote with your feet—assemble in your city square now and sing our National Anthem. I will appear at as many of these meeting as I can this evening. Thank you. And please pray for our Sweden."

No one in the room spoke.

Finally the interviewer said, "You're an atheist, aren't you?"

"I am, but after this afternoon I am hedging my bets."

No one laughed.

A moment later a knock on the door announced the arrival of Johansson's car.

Turning to the young interviewer, Johansson asked, "Want to come with me?"

"Certainly," was all interviewer could manage.

Thirty minutes later they were in the party's helicopter.

From 6 p.m. and for the next 13 hours, the politician and the young reporter visited 32 city squares. At each, Johansson's message was the same—this is not about parties, this is about the survival of Sweden, and in the large picture, about the survival of Europe.

The election had already been scheduled for September.

Some firebrands in the party suggested that Johansson try to bring it forward.

He shook his head, "That would not be fair."

As he expected, the actions of Mr. Hoodoa and his cohorts were not easily forgotten, played as it was 167 million times a month on HyperTube.

By the close of polling day, Mr. Johansson was the new Prime Minister of Swedish, with a staggering 61% of the popular vote.

●

The story in German-speaking Europe followed much the same path as that of Sweden, only half a decade later. The Germans had been far more leery of immigrants than the Swedes; the Swedes saw themselves as the rightful (and often righteous) guardians of the Enlightenment; the Germans saw the Swedes as weak-kneed fools.

As one self-professed "wise old bird" in Berlin had so rightly reminded his viewers on the old Internet of those days: "You can call me any despicable name you like, but blacks from Africa are simply not the equal of Germans. They are intellectually inferior to whites and Japanese; they are unsophisticated and more like animals than humans. Yes, they have a glorious sense of rhythm, but they are—in the final analysis—simply extremely muscular simpletons, generally incapable of higher learning. The few that do make it to university, do so simply by the virtue of their white genes and by acting as white people. The natural idiom of the African black is sloth, sloth that mandates criminality. Now you can decide what you want for your German children and grandchildren—to suffer the nightmare of Sweden, or to face reality, however unpleasant, and to do that most fearful of all acts: to grow up and view the world as an adult."

This was a point the Berlin politician hammered home for the next three years: that white Europeans had deluded themselves that they were being superior human beings by treating the African migrants as poor people who Fate had treated terribly, and that with more government aid, these African migrants would become the same as the white Europeans, just with a healthy, chocolate-colored skin. This is what the German schools had taught and these schools had used the War of '39 as a convenient excuse.

The problem was it was not true. More and more African migrants and Mohammedans had flooded Europe. All the while, the passive and weak and mild white European politicians all curried favor with their own voters, as well as the migrants by pretending that government could solve all the problems, and that the problems were indeed minor—just temporary bumps in the road. The European elite saw themselves as superior beings, and providing this modern day *noblesse oblige* was proof of this.

●

Sadly, reality's dour face entered—with more and more government aid the migrants bought more and more ganja. And the more polite the police were, the more rapes the Africans committed—the most egregious case was when a wolf pack of nine African migrants stole a van and chased a school bus from a girls' school returning from an outing to the Stockholm Gallery of Fine Arts. It was just before 5 p.m. when the van forced the bus off the road. In under 30 seconds, the Africans had coshed the driver and two of the four female teachers. All 32 girls and the two conscious teachers were raped repeatedly. Most were sodomized as well. One of the two teachers plaintively asked why?

"Why, bitch. You ask why white bitch? Simple bitch. Because we can. And forget about locking your doors. Us niggers are everywhere and we love tight white clean pussy like you and your little girls. Bitch, this country of yours is totally fucked, just like you got fucked in the ass today. Totally."

Six months later, five of the girls had killed themselves as had both of the teachers.

One of the teachers left a note, stained with tears.

"I am sorry to do this, but since the attack my life is one only of fear. I wake up in the morning frightened. I go to work at school frightened. I come home frightened. I sleep with the same terrible nightmare, night after night. My life consists solely of fear. I am sorry, but I have lost the will to fight this fear."

It was with this backdrop that the German One Voice came to become the largest party in German-speaking Europe. As with the other countries of northern Europe, the party's platform was simple: that any and all migrants had to both speak fluent German and have a real job.

12

THE RISE AND RISE OF U.S. PRESIDENT SEBASTIÁN LÓPEZ

By Peter Johnson
The Canadian Institute of Political Studies
Monday, 3 June 2041

OF ALL THE PRESIDENTS IN THE HISTORY of the old United States, and the new Greater United States, President Sebastián López Jr. is likely most unlikely.

President López did not go to Harvard; he did not attend Stanford; and he does not have an MBA from Wharton. Son of a small-town drug dealer, gun runner and part-time informant for the American DEA, what he has instead is the undying loyalty of the mayors of the four largest cities in the United States: Los Angeles, San Diego, San Antonio, and San José. Three of four of these mayors were themselves born in the former Mexico, while the fourth, Juan Ramos is the ninth child of Mexican immigrants living in San Diego.

The old Anglo press often used to refer to them as the "Four Mayors Of The Apocalypse." Once these English-language newspapers were "suspended indefinitely," the term made its way online.

With the support of these four mayors, López was able to make an initial splash on the national stage. Lopez's strategy was high-risk and explosive—he only spoke Spanish for all his campaigning. And when he was asked a question in English by a member of the press corp, he would always answer in Spanish. The reason he stated was "The Latino in America was the negro of the past one hundred years, now it is time for the Latino to take his rightful place. As American politicians speak only English, I believe I have a duty from God to speak only Spanish and to try to change the balance, a balance that is grossly distorted against the god-fearing and family-oriented, humble Latinos."

●

In the early days of his campaign the establishment ridiculed this posturing, and it made many old-time Latino politicians nervous, schooled as they were in the language of compromise and of gradualism. But after the first three primary caucuses in New Mexico, Arizona, and most especially Texas, the direction of the wind changed, and the momentum was behind López.

López's wife, María José, the former Miss Mexico, proved to be a huge asset—immensely popular with the Latina. It was rumored that she was also very much a northern Eva Peron—who she couldn't convince with her intellect, she would persuade with her womanly charms. And as her intellect was widely known to be of a modest dimension, her body was often called into use.

The World Council for Peace had requested Canada provide 500 observers to monitor the election as there had been widespread rumors among the U.S. Anglo expats in Canada of election fraud in past U.S. elections, as this had come to the notice of the WCP. Naturally, as is always the case, the U.S. bridled at the suggestion of any possibility of improprieties, but when the WCP mentioned a possible suspension of WCP support for the enfeebled U.S. Dollar, trading as it was at nine to the Yen, the U.S. reluctantly agreed.

●

As it happens, this precaution was prescient—the corruption was now systemic. Old timers looked backed with rose colored glasses at the campaigns of 2032 and 2036, which were scrupulous in their cleanliness. These two campaigns together represented the apotheoses of American democracy.

Not surprisingly the worst city—and there were over 50 that were judged as "Unacceptable"—was Chicago. Dating back even before the rigged election of 1960, Chicago had the dubious distinction of being the most dishonest city in voting records since records began in 1900. In the recent presidential election, only 13% of eligible black votes cast a vote. While this anomaly has not been fully analyzed, some rumors suggest that the powerful "20 and Eight" gang had been employed to prevent black citizens from voting. It was the "20 and Eight" gang that used black street hoodlums to distribute the narcotics from the Iron Triangle.

13

PEARLS BEFORE SWINE: PIGS AND THE COLLAPSE OF COMMUNIST CHINA

By Hiroki Nakamura, Ph.D.
Tokyo Institute for Advanced Study
Thursday, 4 July 2041

IN 1895, THE WAR BETWEEN JAPAN AND CHINA was decided by the Chinese soldiers' lack of ammunition for their rifles—the Chinese quartermaster had requisitioned the monies to buy whores and opium.

In 2014, the Chinese Army quartermaster was cashiered for spending 400 million U.S. dollars on whores and private palaces.

The more things change, the more things stay the same?

More recently and in a similar manner, the sudden and unexpected collapse of communist China had its roots in this same Chinese trait, but with an interesting twist.

●

The collapse of communist China had been predicted ever since the first year following the communist "takeover" in 1949—there was really no takeover, as in reality, there was little or nothing to takeover.

Until 2032 the Communist Party was able to maintain its dominance. True, there were the occasional bumps in the road: the Tiananmen Square massacre; the 2017 street shooting in the Central District of Hong Kong by the PLA of the 317 of the Umbrella protestors; the 2024 drone attacks in eastern China that killed an estimated 1,700 people (graphically and gleefully shown by the NSA satellite footage on the old YouTube channel). But overall, the party bumbled along, with its charming delight in early Stalinist pantomime—the requisite dyed black hair; the mass rallies of the faithful introduced in 2017; the new Five Daily Freedoms introduced in 2021; and in 2024 the new national anthem that became *comme il faut* at the start of every day everywhere.

But in early 2032, the single entry known as China collapsed in 39 days, like a black star eating itself. In less time than it took the Germans to destroy the French in 1940, the country of China evaporated from the face of the planet to be replaced by a loose confederation of ever-bickering modern-day cantons. But this apparent suddenness was actually decades in the making. And it all started in Argentina in the early 1990s...

●

In early 1991, Argentinean ranchers started to chop down thousands of hectares of forest; they also pushed their traditional cattle-breeding from the Pampas to remote areas.

Why?

Soybeans.

Or more specifically, soybeans for Chinese pigs. And these creatures lived up to their reputation and name—each kilogram of a pig's body weight required six kilograms of feed, and feed moreover consisted mostly of soybeans, soybeans from South America, mostly Argentina. The last herd statistics were from 2029, and they described an estimated Chinese herd of 1,700 million animals (87% of the world's pig population). In the years 1990 to 2030, the Argentinean soybean production increased 16-fold, and exports topped out in 2030 at 31m tonnes.

But the appalling destruction of the Argentinian forests was the least of the troubles. And it was the direct connection of the Argentinean farming methods that led to the collapse of the old China. On the 78 million hectares of genetically modified soybean, the Argentinean farmers poured an estimated 950 million liters of pesticides and herbicides. And these were almost exclusively glyphosate-based. The first signs of trouble appeared in Argentina itself in 2005 when the percentage of birth defects to infants born in the Children's Hospital in Cordoba started to skyrocket. Even in those early days—as early as 2005—the main cause of death for children in Cordoba less than one year old was malformation, not malnutrition. At the time, the American EPA standard for glyphosate was 0.7 ppm (parts per million), while the stricter European standard was 0.2 ppm. Blood samples from expectant mothers in Cordoba showed concentrations of up to 198 ppm.

But it was not the massive increase of birth defects in faraway South America that caused the collapse of China. It was that the Chinese pig farms further increased the toxicity of the soybean feed by adding their own lethal cocktail of antibiotics. Here's how it was done.

●

Since wild pigs were first domesticated in southern China 10,000 years ago, Chinese farms have always tried to game the system—they tried just about anything to increase the pig's weight at the stockyard sale. The mostly widely used approach was the simple, but highly effective expedient of jamming a garden hose down the pig's throat and adding ten liters of water to gain ten kilograms.

Obviously, this approach only last an hour or so. Over the past 30 years, what the always-industrious Chinese pig farmers resorted to was to use ever-increasing amounts of growth hormones along with antibiotics, and they did this with the same enthusiasm as Edith Piaf singing at *Chez Marguerite*—the main Gestapo brothel in Paris, just down the street from the Gestapo headquarters.

When mixed with the poisonous soybean feed from South America this created pigs that were bigger and softer while at the same time more and more frail. The tragedy of young mothers in Cordoba started to play out in China, but only 100 times worse—birth defects in Chinese cities soared; at the same time strange digestive problems were reported in ever-increasing numbers, first in the elderly and then over the next half decade in the general population. Of course the communist masters attempted to hide the horrible statistics—birth defects that were 500 times (not percent), 500 times greater than in Europe.

It is not coincidental that the large pig farmers started to build their slaughterhouses at the actual farms. To the outside observer, this seemed to make no business sense. It was the Japanese High Atmosphere Ozone Research Program that stumbled onto the reason. In a chance analysis of the satellite images by the Hitachi supercomputers, some "Non Recognizable Animal Forms" were detected. The images showed dead pigs being moved in open trucks. What had puzzled the computer was that these pigs had six or eight or even ten legs. So, the purpose of the newly established slaughterhouses was to keep this secret by slaughtering the mutant dead animals without any outsiders knowing—"bacon is bacon" was the farmers' common refrain.

When the Japanese published these images and a description of the possible causes, the Chinese government took the unprecedented step of first suspending and then terminating all diplomatic relations with Japan. The world was shocked at these extreme actions by the Chinese over a seemingly minor—indeed trivial—report by the scientists of the Japanese High Atmosphere Ozone Research Program. However, this hysterical reaction turned out to be just the beginning.

●

What the world at large did not know at the time was that the old Chinese Communist government was all too well aware of the problem and that the Japanese had inadvertently hit the rawest of nerves. Of course the Stalinist reaction by the Chinese was the worst possible action, as it simply alerted scientists and governments worldwide to look more closely.

●

The cause of the alarming rise in the fatality rates of the elderly across China took only three weeks to discover. Unfortunately knowing the cause and doing something about it are two very different things. As with the frightening rise of Chinese birth defects, the increased elder fatality rate had the same source: South America.

One of the most insidious effects of glyphosate is its effects on human intestinal microflora. These microflora are silent partners in the operation of the digestion in mammals and are essential to keep pathogens in check. One of the most common—and one of the most dangerous—of these pathogens is Clostridium Botulinum, commonly called "botulism." In a noted study, German researchers found that specific intestinal bacteria manufacture bacteriocines that destroy

Clostridium Botulinum. Unfortunately these essential bacteria are destroyed by even the slightest trace of glyphosate.

The problem became how to "reseed" the stomach of the elderly once the glyphosate had taken its toll. In a normal and healthy adult this would have been relatively easy, but the problem arose with the glyphosate already in the patient's system because every time a dose of intestinal microflora was given it was destroyed by the glyphosate. Moreover, botulism mortality is high and it is fast moving. According to reports smuggled out by European doctors working in Chinese hospitals, the mortality rate for this man-made epidemic of Clostridium Botulinum in China was not the typical 5% but was closer to 25%. (Two French doctors in Shanghai who were so unwise as to speak—on the record—to an Agence France-Presse reporter, were summarily tried in secret and convicted on the same day for "divulging state secrets"—the classic Chinese Communist tactic for any and all dissidents from Nobel winners to the humble high school *student* who posted her class's examination result online.)

●

Monday, the last day of June 1924 was a swelteringly hot day in Washington with a humidity reading of over

90% and the temperature of over 95 degrees in the shade, if any shade could be found. A little after noon, defying the heat, two young men could be seen on the White House tennis court, reveling in the heat and the passionate, if somewhat uneven, game of tennis.

Young Calvin Coolidge Jr. was secretly delighted to be playing with his older brother John. The unevenness of the game in no way dampened young Calvin enthusiasm. In fact, Calvin was so eager that hot Monday that he had rushed to dress and in the process skipped putting on socks.

Hour after hour the two boys delighted in hitting the white tennis balls back and forth. It wasn't until almost four that they stopped, with Calvin limping from a blister on his right foot. Neither thought anything of it. Eight days later, young Calvin Coolidge Jr. was dead.

Nothing could be done to stop the fatal blood poisoning of the favorite son of the most powerful man in the world—there were no antibiotics.

●

Today, in 2041, a world without antibiotics is unimaginable. The loss of the ability to use antibiotics would be to set the clock back 120 years to 1924; routine surgery like hip replacements would become life-threatening; common robotic organs transplants would be impossible.

And yet this is precisely what the farmers of the world are moving towards.

In his 1945 Nobel Prize Winner's lecture Sir Alexander Fleming said, *"It is not difficult to make microbes resistant to penicillin in the laboratory by exposing them to concentrations not sufficient to kill them and the same thing has occasionally happened in the body."* It became a standard exercise for undergraduates in microbiology to produce antibiotic-resistant bacteria in the laboratory. Within 72 hours the resistant population is in the hundreds of billions.

●

The worst offenders—by far—in this high-risk game of poker were the Chinese pig farmers, for whom any action to increase profits was deemed acceptable, even admirable. The extreme case of profit over safety that is still cited today was the horrific story of the Chinese dairy in 2008 which deliberately adulterated milk with toxic melamine—a plastic that is flame retardant and often used in the manufacture of counter tops. It is the 67% of the nitrogen in melamine that makes it so effective as a flame retardant. But this same nitrogen also has a more sinister use—to spike the protein levels in milk; the two common tests—the Kjeldahl and Dumas methods—both simply measure the protein levels (via the nitrogen concentration) and cannot tell the source. So nitrogen from melamine and the naturally occurring nitrogen in the milk's amino acids are seen as identical. Over 300,000 babies were hospitalized and over 100 died, according to unofficial numbers; the numbers are unofficial because the Chinese government stated at the time, *"because this is not an infectious* [sic] *epidemic, there is no need to release any fatality numbers."*

The profit-at-any-cost approach of the Chinese farmers has meant the ever-increasing use of cheap antibiotics. But, unknown to the Chinese farmers, this was very much a Faustian bargain, for as these farmers increase the antibiotics, so they slowly but ineluctably weaken the herd, and Chinese pig herds these days are extremely incestuous, many herds of 5,000 swine are all half-brothers or half-sisters. The so-called Sevens Epidemics of 2007, 2017, and 2027 all show the egregious dangers of the approach of Chinese pig husbandry. In 2007 an estimated 45 million pigs died of the "blue ear pig disease;" in 2017 it was 14 million; and in 2027 it was a staggering 215 million dead pigs in just under eight months. It was this third and most severe epidemic that showed the first crack in the Chinese communist party's defense of this politically-essential staple.

•

To attempt to ameliorate the effects of these man-made epidemics as well as actual natural disasters, the party established a pork Reserve—a huge bureaucracy of frozen pork and live pigs to act as a reserve capacity to help balance supply and demand; when supply was high and consequently prices weakened, the Reserve would buy excess capacity to maintain the farmers' profits; when supply was low and prices high, the Reserve would release some of its reserves to the pig wholesalers.

At least that was the theory.

As with the war of 1895, the devil was in the details. What actually happened was a shell game that would have impressed even the most hardened New York hustler in Washington Square Park. Rather than taking delivery of the physicals, the Reserve would simply make a bookkeeping annotation, making for truly honest graft in the hallowed tradition of Boston Mayor Honey Fitz. So, while reports to the mandarins in Beijing all looked upright and spiffy, the reality was a little less so.

For example, in 2029 the Reserve's reports to Beijing told of 700 million pork bellies being added to the 12 huge refrigerated warehouses dotted across China.

The reality was a little more prosaic: of the 12 巨大的 猪冷冻仓库 (Huge Frozen Pig Warehouses), two actually existed, and they were far smaller than the bosses in the capital were happy to believe had been built. But— at least for the time being—all was smooth and the bosses did not feel inclined to ask too many questions, as it was they were each getting a whole hog each week, courtesy of the Reserve—"it must be working as I get a whole hog each week." They were, to torture a metaphor, pigs in clover.

What actually happened was the Reserve would kick back 10% to the farmers and an additional 20% for "administrative duties" to the local party leader. When the scheme finally unraveled in 2032, one local party leader had amassed a fortune in seven private banks along Switzerland's Bahnhofstrasse of over 27 billion U.S. Dollars; not million, billion. But, as so often happens it China, this lucky apparatchik was ignored and the standard staple was trotted out—evil foreign powers spreading false rumors about China and her people.

But rumors were one thing, no pork was another. As the word in Mandarin for pork is the same as for meat, the intertwining of pork with the Chinese national psyche is clear, and empty meat counters harked all the way back to the bad-old-days of 1949 and the later famines where Mao killed 30 million people.

14

THE EMASCULATION OF THE AMERICAN MALE BY ESTROGENIC POISONING

By Isao Shimizu, MD, Ph.D.
Osaka University Research Hospital
Friday, 2 August 2041

ONE OF THE MOST NOTABLE DIFFERENCES that emerged at the start of this century was the marked difference in the level of male homosexuality in the United States when compared to Japan.

Now-discredited American social commenters arrogantly and wrongly proclaimed this as a sign of Japan's "backwardness"—a "narrow-minded and outdated view of contemporary human sexuality" was a common sneer.

It was the pioneering work done by my colleagues at Osaka University Research Hospital that proved the Americans completely wrong—it was not social, it was chemical.

●

In the past sixty years, study after study showed that American men's testosterone levels had been plummeting. Twenty-five years ago in 2015, the New England Research Institute in Watertown, Massachusetts found that the rate of decease of testosterone in males was 1% per year—a truly catastrophic situation. In real terms this meant that a man in 2002 would have nearly a 15% lower level of testosterone than a man of the same age in 1987.

●

In conjunction with the FACOM Advanced Computer Center in Tokyo, my colleagues proved that it was the massive amount of growth hormones in American meat and other foods, along with the near-universal use of glyphosate and phthlate in the United States that essentially created a perfect food to turn American men into women.

Of the earlier studies our team examined before designing the analysis experiment was the study of 196 boys that had measured phthlate levels in pregnant women and the masculinity of their sons. The masculinity was measured using the universal AGD measurement. The results were startling and the extraordinarily high correlation gave us food for thought.

•

Another observation about livestock production in the United States was that profit always trumped caution. So while European and especially Japanese standards for feed additives were comprehensive and cautious, the Americans seemed to be hell bent on taking precisely the opposite approach with an arrogance that now, in retrospect, was clearly calamitous.

Until the groundbreaking report of 2019 (which won my colleagues the Nobel Medicine prize that year), there had been some desultory and mostly ineffective boycotts of meat imported from the United States; Japanese housewives quietly avoided American meat, while the South Koreans were typically more rambunctious with mass—and sometimes violent— demonstrations in Seoul. Nevertheless, most of these actions and demonstrations were based on hearsay and gossip—there was little hard scientific evidence.

All this changed in March 2019 when the final report was released.

This report proved that the practices of American factory farms were effectively emasculating American men—they were inadvertently being made less masculine and more feminine by the food they were consuming over their lifetime. Some of these changes took effect even before they were born, such as the study mentioned above, while other changes were extremely gradual, taking decades. But the sum effect was a pronounced and easily measured decrease in masculine traits in American men—from testosterone levels to AGD measurements.

It was this chemical pollution—rather than populist New Age gobbledygook—that was the difference in the levels of male homosexuality in the United States when compared to Japan. Because of the strict food standards that have always been in effect in Japan, Japanese men continued to maintain normal and healthy levels of testosterone. In fact, the T-levels in Japanese men at the time of writing (2041) are significantly higher than the T-levels of any other nation.

While much has been made of this in the emergence of Japan as notionally "the World's Only Superpower," in the opinion of this scientist this dominance is more likely related to the superior Japanese education system—the second-best education system today is that of Greater Germany, and not coincidentally, Greater Germany is the second largest economy in the world after Japan.

15

THE 2020/2/20 CAMPAIGN: JAPAN FINALLY STANDING PROUD

By Shigeo Yamamoto
Kobe Center of Political Research
Thursday, 5 September 2041

TODAY IN 2041 IT IS HARD TO BELIEVE that it was just twenty years ago that there were still American occupation forces in Japan.

While nominally the American forces in Japan were described as "providing stability for the region," this was simply a thread-bare lie, trotted out by the Americans and their long-suffering supporters in the LDP party. The real reason—that the Americans were so eager to hide—was to be able to continue bullying Japan. The best example of this leverage was the Plaza Accord of 1985. This accord was touted as "pro-growth," and there was some truth to this as it was very pro-growth for the United States but at the expense of Japan; with all the American troops in Japan at the time, the Japanese had little option but to agree.

●

Ironically it was from some renegades in the self-same LDP that the campaign which became known as 2020/2/20 started. This was the date to have all American occupation forces purged from Japan. Not surprisingly, it started in Okinawa, where the main USMC air bases were located—18% of Okinawa was occupied by the American forces.

Traditionally, the U.S. Marines had kept a low profile. Yes, there sometimes was the boorish behavior by some of the American servicemen, but overall there was relative calm, and the Okinawans gritted their teeth and tolerated the presence of these odious foreigners.

●

Unfortunately all this changed on Sunday, the Fourth of August 2019. A new commander had recently taken over the main base at Futenma, and he reversed his predecessor's policy of limited and low-key liberty from the base. In the past, only a very small number of foreigners were allowed off the base at any one time. But the new commander—one of the most senior black commanders in the Marines—thought this needlessly restrictive and he felt that his men should be allowed, even had the right, to frequent any establishment in any numbers. But this new approach proved to be disastrous—rather than small and well-behaved groups of four or five, the new policy allowed groups of up to 500 servicemen into Futenma.

●

One of the most significant changes in America in the ten years leading up to 2019 was the rapid and extensive polarization of American society. Not by any direct policy or law, the Ellis-Island tradition of assimilation slowed and then reversed. For 150 years, the most important part of the American Dream was to become American. That meant assimilation. But starting in the 1980s, and accelerating in the decade preceding 2019, American society became more and more fragmented into African-American, Spanish-American, Chinese-American, and so on, so that national origin and race became the primary factor. This in turn led to the creation of modern-day ghettos.

Ghettos originated in Renaissance Venice as the part of the city where Jews were segregated. While the Jewish ghetto in Venice was relatively affluent, other Italian Jewish ghettos were extremely poor and squalid, as was the case in the Jewish Ghetto in Rome. Often

Jews in these ghettos were prohibited from leaving during the Christian festivals of Christmas and Easter.

Especially for African-Americans, the modern day ghettos in American cities lead to a decrease in services and security—critical life-saving services, such as fire and ambulance services, would only enter some areas during daylight, and only with heavily-armed police escorts. When combined with the massive increase in black illegitimacy, the hyper-violent Wolfie (q.v.) phenomenon became the rule and not the exception in these modern ghettos.

It was only learned in 2022 that the American forces in Japan had an overall "waiver rate" of 16% and among blacks it was 36%. A waiver is needed when a recruit would otherwise be rejected as "unfit for service." There are many reasons a waiver may be needed. In some cases it is a physical disability, such as poor eyesight; in some cases it is because of a mental limitation, such as low IQ; in some cases it is because of a personality issue, such as lack of respect for authority or a penchant for violence. An earlier, notable waiver was the one granted to Sgt. Bergdahl by the U.S. Army after he had earlier been discharged for the U.S. Coast Guard after 26 days of the 180-day basic training. He was discharged from the Coast Guard with an "uncharacterized discharge."

All the American armed services increasingly mirrored civilian society. Just as in the American prisons, the armed services became more and more structured along racial lines. It was one of these groups of 200 to 500 black servicemen (accounts of the actual numbers vary widely depending on who was asked), that ran riot that hot August night in Futenma. It took all the local Japanese Futenma police and the base's security force to restore order in the weeks following 4 August 2019.

After calm returned, nine Japanese were dead. The most egregious incident was when a mother and her two teenage daughters were set upon by one of these Wolfie splinter groups. Somehow, shots were fired by one or more of the drunk servicemen and the three Japanese women lay dead. Precisely what happened is still unknown.

Not surprisingly, the Japanese were outraged. To make matters much worse, the new commander refused point blank to allow the Japanese to try the suspects. For the Japanese, this was a stark reminder of the comments of Admiral Macke in the aftermath of the 1995 rape by three black servicemen of a 12-year-old Japanese school girl when Macke said, "*I think it was absolutely stupid. I have said several times: for the price they paid to rent the car [used in the crime], they could have had a girl [prostitute]."*

And it was the memory of this infamous rape that rekindled the bitter feeling towards the foreign U.S. military presence. This, in conjunction with the general high-handedness whenever the U.S. military was dealing with the many incidents of accidents on Japanese soil.

One such incident was the accident when a U.S. Marine Corps transport helicopter that crashed on the campus of the Okinawa International University in August 2004. In this case, the Americans cordoned off the area and prevented access by the Japanese police investigators, in spite of the campus being on Japanese sovereign soil.

●

After the uproar caused by the Americans' handling of the August riot, one shocking fact emerged from the Japanese police interrogations. And it answered one question: for five years the Futenma had been puzzled by the deaths of a number of elder Japanese men who had been killed with a single blow to the head. After much questioning and cross-checking, the Futenma police discovered a gang of servicemen who called themselves the "Williamsburg Crew." This small group of seven black servicemen had concocted a horrible and bizarre so-called game called "knockout" where gang members would stalk an unsuspecting Japanese man and would then deliver a single, terrifying blow to the face. According to a youth violence expert, Professor Charles Williams, *That's America. America loves violence and so do our kids. We market violence to our children and we wonder why they're violent. It is because we are.* The mobile telephones of three of the seven suspects contained photographs of the dead Japanese victims.

●

The American whitewash of the investigation of the August riot infuriated the Japanese, as did the discovery of the "Williamsburg Crew." Japanese politicians of all political persuasions joined as one, and this, more than anything, gave the 2020/2/20 campaign the boost it needed. Japanese chat shows spoke of nothing but the 2020/2/20 campaign. It became *de rigueur* for all Japanese politicians to wear the red and yellow arm bands of the campaign.

16

BRIDGESTONE STARS

By Satoshi Ito
Tokyo Gastronomy Institute
Thursday, 17 October 2041

THE WORLD'S LARGEST TIRE COMPANY was formed in 2035 with the purchase of Michelin by Bridgestone. Bridgestone used the purchase to rapidly extend its sales of its nylon-based tire for electric cars, which now represent 92% of all new car sales in Japan, 76% in the United States, and 34% in the New China Confederacy. These new tires were so popular and so fashionable that owners of old, traditional black tires were known to paint their black tires with light blue neon paint to attempt to mimic the new, hip tires.

A significant change that also took place was the renaming of the venerable Michelin stars for restaurant ratings. The famed "Red Book" was started in 1900 by Michelin as a way to encourage well-to-do Parisians to use their new automobiles (and thus wear out the tires). In 2035, the guide's name was changed to the "Bridgestone Michelin Restaurant and Hotel Guide." As this was a mouthful, the guide's name was changed in 2037 to the simpler "Bridgestone Guide."

Of course, the French kicked up a fuss about yet-another of their "cultural heritages" being sold off. This time the demonstrations and complaints were muted. This was in direct contrast to the sales of the Louvre and the Eiffel Tower to Greater Germany in a two-week period in May 2030, after the Germans refused unequivocally to support the New Franc, which had plummeted 37% in three days against the Reich Mark.

The Germans quietly enjoyed the spectacle of the French squirming. When the Minister of Finance, Hermann Graf Schwerin von Krosigk, was heard to comment on an open microphone, *"we've completed what my grandfather's generation started 90 years ago in May 1940,"* there was an immediate uproar by the French, who expected a groveling apology. Instead, the Greater German Chancellor simply cancelled the talks between the German and French finance departments. It was this act the dropped the New Franc by an eye-popping 21% in one afternoon trading session. The next day when the French pleaded with the Germans, the

Chancellor, standing alongside von Krosigk, quietly and briefly read out the terms of support by the Germans of the French currency; the French had 12 hours to respond, otherwise at 09:00 the next day the Germans would no longer support the New Franc in the way they had done for the past decade. Among the properties on the Germans' laundry list were the Louvre and the Eiffel Tower. (It should be remembered that Napoleon's Tomb had been blown to smithereens by the Mohammad Brotherhood in 2025.)

●

It was with this background that the standard French whining and hand-wringing occurred. "*But, at least it was not the Germans this time,*" was the common refrain. In addition, any French complaints had feet of clay, as the following table makes so clear (it should be remembered that the first old-style "Michelin" guide to Tokyo was first published only in 2007, and even in 2007, Tokyo was awarded more stars than Paris).

As early as 2007, Jean-Luc Naret, Michelin's editorial director was unrepentant: "*Tokyo is by far the world's capital of gastronomy.*"

Michael Ellis took over from Naret and his comment—widely reported at the time—was "*Japanese gourmet cooking is even more creative, inspired and inventive than in the past.*" It was the "even more" that caused the firestorm in France. Thoughtful analysts pointed to the slow decline in French cooking: the loss of the traditional brasseries; France has more McDonalds—"Le Big Mac"—per capita than anywhere in the world, including the U.S.

Bridgestone/Michelin Stars

	Tokyo	Paris
2013	323	281
2020	376	299
2025	475	297
2030*	566	176
2035	706	223

* New Franc Currency Crisis

●

Just as Tokyo women today in 2041 are what the smoky and sublimely sexy Parisian women were like in the late 1940s and the early 1950s, Japanese cooking today is what French cooking was in the same period: fanatical dedication to the muse; the best and freshest ingredients; the unending quest for perfection; presentations that are always perfect.

An example of the Japanese dedication to the craft is the size of the restaurants. Just like in Paris in 1950s, many Japanese restaurants have only eight or ten seats—no McDonald's here. An example of these tiny restaurants is Sushi-Sho, a diminutive restaurant consisting of all of ten seats. The founding chef, 75-year-old Keiji Nakazawa was one of Japan's foremost experts on sushi. Each patron was told where each fish was caught—tuna from near Nagasaki; eel from Osaka, etc. And the venerable chef described if fish was caught by line or net.

●

Why the top five car makers in 2041 are all Japanese is illustrated by this fish story: Mr. Nakazawa's successor insists on knowing the depth his fishermen caught the golden eye snapper, because below 200 meters, the water pressure makes the fish's skin too tough. When foreigners show surprise at this level of attention to detail, their Japanese hosts are often puzzled—*"but this is normal for Tokyo,"* they explain to the outsider or "gaijin."

●

It is common for yakitori restaurants to provide a chart so diners can select the part of the bird that they want. And most Tokyo yakitori restaurants use only bincho charcoal—the Rolls Royce of charcoal.

How did Tokyo become the gastronomic capital of the world? The quick answer is, slowly. It took almost a century, starting in the early 1960s. In those days, the allure of French cooking had not yet been destroyed by Le Big Mac and by the French's own dismissive disdain of hard work. In those days, young Japanese journeyed to Paris to learn from the masters, just as young Honda engineers travelled to the Isle of Man to photograph Nortons, Gileras, and the occasional MV. In both cases the results were the same: total Japanese dominance. It is true that the Hondas started their dominance fifty years before the Paris-trained Japanese chefs, but the results were the same: complete annihilation of the once-great Europeans.

●

Attention to detail: it is common for Tokyo restaurants to serve salads consisting of 37 different vegetables, all of which were growing in the earth less than 24 hours ago. Fanatical? Perhaps, but not uncommon for Paris of the 1950s, extinct in the Paris of the 2040s with the daily collapse of the New Franc and the dozens of armored cars permanently stationed on the Champs-Élysées in their feeble attempt to control the Mohammedans who now infest the City of Light, committing petty crimes against the now-rare tourist.

●

Commitment to the future: in direct contrast to Paris, Tokyo in 2041 is overwhelmed by the number of applicants for the limited number of apprenticeships. To quote just one pair of statistics: last year, in 2040, the number of applicants for patisseries in Paris was 21% of the vacancies; in Tokyo for the patisseries it was 1,429%—14 applicants for every opening.

17

JAPANESE ULTRA-PURE FOOD 'PARADISES'

By Akira Yoshida, Ph.D.
Japanese National Food Standards Board (JNFSB)
Monday, 21 October 2041

THE RAPIDLY INCREASING CASES OF ADULTERATED FOOD being imported into Japan at the start of this century prompted the government to expand the scope and gamut of the Japanese National Food Standards Board. It was the case of lettuce imported from the "old China," adulterated with human feces, that outranged Japanese housewives.

Most people do not realize today that the now ubiquitous Japanese Food Paradises were originally created as a research project of JNFSB. The initial name of these production centers was "Food Factories," but even the most hardened bureaucrat realized very quickly that no self-respecting Japanese housewife would ever consider buying food for her family produced in a "factory." So, a name competition was held in the JNFSB offices next to the Imperial Palace; the winner was a 21-year-old office lady, Miki Okino, originally from Osaka, who won the prize of four tickets to Tokyo DisneySea. Her winning suggestion was "Food Paradises," a name the three judged unanimously agreed was the best. So "food factories" became "food paradises."

●

The most important concept of the food paradise was to make Japan self-sufficient in food. The extensive attempts by the Americans to starve Japan to death in the early 1930s had not been forgotten. In addition, the rapidly aging farming population had to be addressed; not only was the farming population aging, but young people in rural areas were fleeing to the big cities, especially Tokyo, to escape the backbreaking stoop labor that all farmers endure; better to be working in a clean and warm Starbucks serving espresso than in the freezing cold of the fields back home.

These factors combined with Japan's growing pre-eminence in robotronics led to the rapid development of the food paradises. Actually, the basic concepts were surprisingly simple: have artificial sunlight shining 24 hours a day, seven days a week; use both hydroponic and traditional soil, but the enhanced soil was a product of the Fiji Soil Company—three times as nutritious as real soil, and over 500 times more pure—no debris of modern society to pollute this soil; and provide purified water that was both nutritious and pure at the same time.

The "sunlight" was light generated from specially developed LEDs by the Toyota Motor Corp. and protected by 47 patents worldwide; this light provided the most perfect light to encourage rapid and natural plant growth—no chemicals or pesticides, just perfect light around the clock. Of course, different vegetables required different Growth Optimization Spectrums—the LEDs used for light-green-colored lettuce were very different from those used for dark-green spinach and broccoli; this differential spectrum constituted over half of the patents.

●

The area of most rapid evolution was the robotronics—in the early food paradise prototypes the plants were harvested with human-like hands that attempted to mimic humans. As is described elsewhere in this yearbook, one of the biggest mistakes that early robotronics engineers made was their slavish attempts to have the early machines mimic humans—akin to Monkey See, Monkey Do. This was a mistake. The correct approach, finally adopted after much trial and error, was to answer the simplest question: how can the lettuce, or carrot, or spinach best be harvested with the least bruising? And it turned out that a thumb and four fingers was one of the least effective ways—humans did it this way in the past for the simple reason they had no alternatives.

●

Obviously a hydroponic food paradise was the easiest case. In a hydroponic paradise the vegetable is grown in a highly nutritious water bath; no soil is used at all. Hydroponic cultivation has a long history dating back to 1627 with a book written by Francis Bacon; in 1699, John Woodward published his experiments with the cultivation of spearmint in water; in 1842 the Germans took the lead when Julius von Sachs and Wilhelm Knop published a list of nine elements they believed essential for the best soil-less cultivation.

Lettuce was the first hydroponic vegetable grown in the Japanese food paradises. After the first five years, the food paradises were all constructed by building robots, so the proliferation and growth of the paradises was extremely rapid: in 2018, just under 1% of all food grown in Japan was produced at a food paradise; by 2028 it was 45%.

Following the pioneering work of Sachs and Knop, the most important question the JNFSB had to answer was what is the optimum combination of trace elements and the type of light? Would a change of the spectrum mandate a change in the mix of trace elements? And if so, how could this be developed?

The elegant solution provided by the JNFSB scientists was to first list the trace elements and the likely upper and lower bounds. Then the possible spectrums to be used were listed. Once the lists were compiled, a robotronics program was created so that in the third basement of the JNFSB in Tokyo, an experiment of over 32,000 permutations was conducted. Each growing area or cell measured 15 centimeters square and was protected on all four sides by blackened aluminum shades to prevent pollution from the adjacent cells. In this way the optimum mix was developed in a little over two weeks. Not surprisingly, these optimum mixes were protected by worldwide patents.

●

There are clearly many benefits of food produced at food paradise. First and foremost, it is grown in Japan under Japanese control—never again could a starvation blockade by America hurt Japan. Second, the food is the purest possible, even by the strict Japanese food standards. More for amusement than for edification, the JNFSB did a comparison of lettuce produced at a

Japanese food paradise with lettuce grown in the new North China Confederation and the United States. The results were as expected: the Chinese food had over 167 times the number of impurities, including—hard though this is to believe—traces of rat poison; the American samples had no rat poison but massive doses (over 1,120 times the Japanese sample) of herbicides including massive amounts of glyphosate known to create birth defects. Third, the growth rate—for a far superior vegetable—was reduced from 70 days to 10 days. Fourth, the "product density" (as JNFSB analysts still insist on calling the growth density) is over nine times that of a traditional farm per level. In other words, on the same area of ground, there are nine times the density of lettuce when compared to traditional open-field cultivation. But this neglects the fact that the robot-built food paradises are typically 16 or 32 layers and each layer is just 1.5 meters in height—no human ever enters a layer.

It is these last two statistics—the growth rate and the growth density—that meant that Japan was exporting food as early as 2031. And the ultra-pure Japanese produce commanded a significant premium over the traditional vegetables produced using massive doses of herbicides.

In summary, the JNFSB is proud to have made Japan a food-exporting country for the first time in history, and is equally proud of leading the way in growing vegetables of unparalleled purity. While the statistical data is still sketchy, it seems that the highly nutritious paradise vegetables, that are now available to all levels of Japanese society, have added two or three years to the average Japanese life expectancy.

18

JAPANESE ECONOMIC DEVELOPMENT PARTNERSHIPS IN 2041: A TOUR D'HORIZON

By Hiroshi Takahashi
Tokyo International Studies Institute
Tuesday, 22 October 2041

AT THE TIME OF WRITING THERE ARE CURRENTLY 17 JEDPs (Japanese Economic Development Partnerships). These range in size from the minuscule to the massive—from the pair of desalination plants in Madagascar to the huge—with an appropriately massive name—the North Western Australian Joint Mining And Exploration Partnership.

Truth be told, none of these agreements are partnerships at all. What they actually are is the use of the Japan's formidable economic power today in 2041 to buy what the Japanese Imperial Army failed to take in 1941.

Of these, the largest one in Australia—with the unwieldy title—is the most controversial. To understand this situation it is worth recalling that the American president Herbert Hoover spent time in northern Australia in the early 1900s as a young mining engineer and referred to the Australian workers collectively as "noodle heads." It was the universal laziness and tendency to drunkenness that drove mad the future "Boy Wonder," creator—along with Roosevelt—of the latest Great Depression.

Fifty years ago—in the 1990s—the Chinese tried and failed to buy a number of large mining properties in the forlorn idea of bringing in cheap Chinese labor, à la the Victorian gold rush of the 1850s. Alas, the Chinese had never bothered to read the Australian labor laws, which severely limited working hours of the worker—regardless of nationality or race. Also, there were massive payment burdens on the employer—free air travel every 28 days; one month in four off with double-time loading pay, et cetera, et cetera. In the end, the Chinese state enterprises threw up their hands and gave up. The only permanent monuments were the vindictive and whining complaints in the Chinese government mouthpiece, the *China Daily* newspaper.

•

When the Japanese Council for Economic Development first proposed the partnership to the Western Australian government in Perth, the state government reacted with alacrity. However, the first steps were dogged with a few missteps: the state government mining minister in charge of the negotiations was heard to boast on a stolen sound bite that "we fucked the Chinese, we sure as well can fuck the Japs as well."

Alas for the minister, the opposite occurred. The trap the Japanese negotiators laid was to insist on using the original Chinese agreement with no changes at all, and only one addition. So flabbergasted where the Western Australians that they barely glanced at the 57-word addition. It seemed harmless—that the Japanese mining company—the Yamato Mining and Trading Corporation—be solely responsible for all security on the Partnership's properties, *in accordance with the existing Western Australian statutes.*

Of course the Australians in Perth were overjoyed with the horrific blunder the Japanese had so obviously made. But the reality was a little different. Before contacting the government in Perth, the first step the Japanese took was to scrutinize the original Chinese agreement; the second step was to review Western Australian case law regarding mining.

As mentioned earlier, the cause of the failure of the Chinese project was the Chinese egregious neglect of reviewing the labor laws for employees and contractors. In contrast to the lackadaisical Chinese, the Japanese had used the Tokyo branch of Baker McKenzie to understand the details of the Western Australian labor laws. The head of the Japanese delegation is reported to have said in the confidential pre-negotiation briefing in Tokyo, *"The Baker report is very good, but it fails to mention the absence of two words, the Baker report describes 'labor laws for employees and contractors.' In fact, it should specify 'labor laws for human employees and human contractors.'"*

And this was the nub of the Japanese strategy, and how the Japanese approach was indeed diametrically opposed to the Chinese one. As always, the Chinese approach was cheap brawn, and as always the Japanese approach was expensive brains.

●

The so-called partnership initially encompassed 9% of the land of Western Australia, and another 2% was later added. As one surprisingly astute Green party member ranted in the Western Australian parliament,

"We have just sold a large chunk of Western Australia to the Japanese."

When told of this comment, the President of Yamato Mining and Trading Corporation—an avid reader of the history of his new fiefdom said, "Not all noodle heads..."

●

And so it came to pass that the Japanese were able to control some of the richest and most valuable mining real estate on the face of the planet. Moreover with complete and absolute control of the security of these vast tracts.

●

The first shock came uncomfortably early to the state government in Perth. The state government mining minister was eager to push the deal forward, mainly as his stepping stone to the premiership. So it was with some little shock and greater concern that he learned of the Japanese plan for security of the properties. The mining minister has introduced the topic of working hours for the security contractors. The Japanese at the meeting looked up in surprise and asked "what contractors?"

The mining minister, now a little less cocky and brash, mentioned the contractors the Chinese had been forced to employ. The Japanese patiently explained that there were to be no contractors, no employees, no actual humans at all for the security.

Now starting to panic the minister—half threatening and half pleading—asked then how security would be provided? The Japanese slowly and carefully laid out the plan of the Yamato company, namely to use no humans; all the security was to be automated, centrally controlled from the Yamato office in Tokyo.

"But what about the promises you made about employing Australian workers?" the minister, now flushing scarlet, demanded. The Japanese team all looked at each other with genuine surprise.

"What Australian workers?" came the polite question from the head of the Japanese delegation.

"All the ones you promised to employ."

The Japanese paused, and then asked, innocently as it turned out, "What promise?"

The Australian minister, now standing, leaned forward and bellowed,

"The promises in the fucking agreement you signed."

Now the Japanese were completely flummoxed. They passed the English version of the agreement to the pig of a minister and asked to be shown where the promise was located in the document.

The minister suddenly slumped in his chair when he realized that he had confused the agreement in front of him with a rough draft of the earlier Chinese agreement.

Blustering, the minister wildly fabricated, "Well it's not actually written but it was a clear understanding. A hand-shake deal, as we western Australians often make."

The minister's own team members were squirming and the leader of the public servants tried to smooth feathers with, "Minister, perhaps it is best if we adjourn for a brief period so we can re-examine the agreement."

Meekly the minister nodded.

This little human comedy occurred at 11:07.

●

By 11:45, the Premier's office had announced the mining minister had "regrettably and with a heavy heart" decided to retire from public life due to "ill health."

As one wag in the press corp had pointed out, "that fat pig's petard has hoisted his own bacon."

●

It was after that stormy meeting that the Australians realized the size of their blunder; a foreign power now had complete and absolute control and sovereignty over nine percent of the entire state, a state four times the size of Texas.

●

Meekly, the Australians chattered among themselves in pubs and bars about how, "the Japs will never make a go of it, without our showing them how..." On this point, the opposite turned out to be the case. Not only did the Yamato corporation "make a go of it," but they did so with no Australians being allowed on their properties.

What the Australians did not know was that the Yamato had been planning these exploits in far-off foreign climes for over a quarter of a century. As early as 2020, Yamato had started initial field work at the old Ashio Copper Mine, in Tochigi prefecture, on the first—and exceptionally crude—versions of the Hydra Robotte system.

The basic principles of the Hydra Robotte have not changed since the early 2020s. Essentially, it consists of nine tiny independent arms or antennas that nibble tiny amounts of soil with the individual antenna's teeth. This soil is passed into a microscopic mass spectrometer located five centimeters from the teeth on the individual arm. The data is then fed to the surface and then in turn to the data center in Tokyo. Apart from the astonishing engineering virtuosity in the creation of the microscopic antennas with their diamond cutters, the other critical breakthrough was the software than combined the inputs from the nine independent antennas.

With surprising speed—averaging up to ten meters an hour—the Hydra Robotte would ride the seam of the mineral, the nine arms all moving independently. Of course this entailed some to'ing and fro'ing as the Robotte would sometimes reverse itself for a few meters when the seam being traced took an unexpected sudden turn, but this did not happen as often as was initially expected—Mother Nature liked flowing seams in all of her minerals.

●

One of the more interesting aspects of the Hydra Robotte that has not previously been described is its use of differential radioactive isotopes as markers— modern day bread crumbs as it were. The design of the Robotte is a two-phase one—first the Robotte traces the seam of interest; in the second phase the actual extractor runs. Whereas the cross-section form factor of each of the nine antennas is less than one square millimeter, the extractor is over nine square meters. While mostly brawn, the extractor's programmed retracing of the Hydra Robotte's trail blazing is verified and re-calibrated by checking the differential isotopes (a differential isotope consists of three different radioactive isotopes that are injected into the soil, but each injection is unique because the ratio of isotopes varies in every case, in essence, a radioactive fingerprint).

●

It was with this bold, but painstakingly tested revolutionary advanced robotics technology that the Yamato Corporation became the world's leading mining company in the space of just 10 years. In retrospect, it was obvious, as all obvious things are in retrospect. In this case of mining, the industry had been crying out for real automation for 150 years.

Until Yamato, the main approach of mining automation had been to make human miners more productive. But the obvious flaw in this approach is that all that it did was to give more power to the noodle heads.

In contrast, the green-field design of the Yamato engineers removed the need for expensive, unreliable, demanding, and lazy human miners—no more noodle heads.

ACKNOWLEDGEMENTS

AS WITH GODDESS, DEAN LEKOS turned turgid, confusing, and obscure prose into something readable.

MISS YOKO ITO also provided additional proofing.

BIBLIOGRAPHICAL NOTES

THE FOLLOWING ARE BOOKS AND ARTICLES that were instrumental in writing *The Last Bastion of Civilization*. The reader can check other facts and quotes by using Google and Wikipedia. All intellectual property is the property of the respective owners.

For your convenience, the links below are also available at **www.AndrewBlencowe.com** to enable easier access to these notes.

If the reader believes the above yarn far-fetched, then viewing the following short 14-minute film will likely be enlightening:

https://www.youtube.com/watch?v=bXn1xavynj8

Made by a young film maker and her exceptionally courageous actress, it shows the raw underbelly of America—today—in 2015.

COMPARED WITH

https://www.youtube.com/watch?v=QQ16XqAc2Ck

ANDREW BLENCOWE

INTRODUCTION

Colvin, Ian Goodhope. *The Chamberlain Cabinet.* New York: Taplinger Pub. Co., 1971

"The greatest phenomenon of mass rape in history..."

Beevor, Antony. *The Fall of Berlin 1945.* New York: Viking, 2002.

Why is there no looting in Japan?

http://blogs.telegraph.co.uk/news/edwest/100079703/why-is-there-no-looting-in-japan/

"Historical narratives of violent pasts have always been useful instruments for politicians to legitimise existing orders or to try and forge national identities," writes Maarten Van Alstein of the Flemish Peace Institute...

http://www.economist.com/news/international/21610241-how-britains-former-dominions-remember-war-propelled-them-independence

THE RISE OF THE JAPANESE SUPER STATE: 2010 TO 2040

But a crucial one has to be that the average affluent child now receives 6,000 hours more enrichment activity—for example, being read to, taken to a museum, coached in a sport or other kind of stimulation provided by adults—than the average poor child, and this gap has greatly increased since the 1970s...

http://in.reuters.com/article/2014/06/09/us-summers-inequality-idINKBN0EK17C20140609

Japan has one of the world's best-educated populations... The high school dropout rate is about 2%...

http://japanese.about.com/od/japaneselessons/a/061000.htm

COMPARED WITH

Some Counties in California See More Than 30% of Students Drop Out...

http://www.kidsdata.org

Arthur Herman: Japan's coming drone revolution

http://asia.nikkei.com/magazine/20141002-
REINVENTING-THE-MALL/Tech-Science/
Arthur-Herman-Japan-s-coming-drone-revolution

Putnam begins his analysis with a vignette of his home town of Port Clinton, Ohio, where he graduated from high school in 1959. He notes that while there were class differences then, there was a much higher degree of social equality: children of the wealthiest families in town befriended kids from working-class backgrounds. This equality was underpinned by a critical social reality: virtually everyone, rich or poor, grew up in a two-parent family in which fathers had steady jobs. He then fast-forwards to the present, where deindustrialization has led to a social transformation in which the proportion of children born to unwed parents rose to 40 percent, while drug use and crime became rampant. In the meantime, a new tier of luxury gated communities has appeared on the nearby shores of Lake Erie...

http://www.ft.com/intl/cms/s/0/6b7cd1f0-c1c1-11e4-
bd24-00144feab7de.html

A 2012 study comparing 16-to-65-year-olds in 20 countries found that Americans rank in the bottom five in numeracy...

> http://www.nytimes.com/2014/07/27/magazine/why-do-americans-stink-at-math.html?_r=0

Rising Illegitimacy: America's Social Catastrophe

> http://www.heritage.org/research/reports/1994/06/rising-illegitimacy

R**3: ROBOTS BUILDING ROBOTS BUILDING ROBOTS, A COLLOQUIAL HISTORY

"Digital nose" on a chip can sniff out diseases

> http://edition.cnn.com/2014/12/19/tech/innovation/digital-nose-disease-breathalyzer/

ENDING THE NORTH CHINA CONFEDERATION'S DROUGHT

Pollution Rising, Chinese Fear for Soil and Food

> http://www.nytimes.com/2013/12/31/world/asia/good-earth-no-more-soil-pollution-plagues-chinese-countryside.html?_r=0

Northern China is running out of water, but the government's remedies are potentially disastrous...

> http://www.economist.com/news/china/21587813-northern-china-running-out-water-governments-remedies-are-potentially-disastrous-all

THE LAST BASTION OF CIVILIZATION

Water in China

http://www.economist.com/news/
leaders/21587789-desperate-measures

China admits widespread soil pollution in 'state secret' report

http://www.ft.com/intl/cms/s/0/c250bd4c-c6b4-11e3-
9839-00144feabdc0.html#axzz3aYbAmRiy

SEE ALSO:

http://www.bloomberg.com/news/articles/2013-10-28/
cancer-express-carries-sufferers-of-india-s-deadly-waters

HYPER VIOLENCE IN AMERICA: THE "WOLFIE" PHENOMENON

"The 'Knockout' Game, a.k.a. 'Polarbearing,' Is a Terrifying Teen Trend"

http://nymag.com/daily/intelligencer/2013/11/knockout-
game-terrifying-teen-trend.html

THE DESIGN CONCEPTS OF THE F89 HYPER FIGHTER

Elephant in your lap: Flying in an F-16

http://edition.cnn.com/2014/11/07/travel/
fly-with-air-force-thunderbirds/

PEARLS BEFORE SWINE: PIGS AND THE COLLAPSE OF COMMUNIST CHINA

Corruption in China's Military Begins With Buying a Job

http://www.bloomberg.com/news/articles/2014-07-01/
chinese-families-pay-16-000-for-kids-to-pass-army-
entrance-exam

Empire of the pig—China's insatiable appetite for pork is a symbol of the country's rise. It is also a danger to the world.

http://www.economist.com/news/christmas-specials/21636507-chinas-insatiable-appetite-pork-symbol-countrys-rise-it-also?fsrc=rss

Can we avoid an antibiotic apocalypse?

http://www.ft.com/intl/cms/s/2/8be857b4-5d3d-11e3-81bd-00144feabdc0.html

The antibiotics that could kill you

http://edition.cnn.com/2014/04/22/opinion/blaser-antibiotic-winter/

Antibiotics resistance "as big a risk as terrorism"—medical chief

http://www.bbc.com/news/health-21737844

THE EMASCULATION OF THE AMERICAN MALE BY ESTROGENIC POISONING

The average levels of the male hormone dropped by 1 percent a year, Dr. Thomas Travison and colleagues from the New England Research Institutes in Watertown, Massachusetts, found. This means that, for example, a 65-year-old man in 2002 would have testosterone levels nearly 15 percent lower than those of a 65-year-old in 1987. This also means that a greater proportion of men in 2002 would have had below-normal testosterone levels than in 1987.

http://www.washingtonsblog.com/2012/04/man-up-boost-your-testosterone-level-for-health-power-and-confidence.html

A glyphosate-based herbicide induces necrosis and apoptosis in mature rat testicular cells in vitro, and testosterone decrease at lower levels.

http://www.ncbi.nlm.nih.gov/pubmed/22200534

Roundup and Glyphosate Toxicity Have Been Grossly Underestimated

http://articles.mercola.com/sites/articles/
archive/2013/07/30/glyphosate-toxicity.aspx

Prenatal Phthalate Exposures and Anogenital Distance in Swedish Boys

http://ehp.niehs.nih.gov/1408163/

BPA May Lower Men's Testosterone, Study Finds

http://www.huffingtonpost.com/2013/05/09/bpa-
testosterone-bisphenol-a-_n_3246042.html

Relationship between urine bisphenol—A level and declining male sexual function

http://www.ncbi.nlm.nih.gov/pubmed/20467048

Endocrine disruptors in bottled mineral water: Estrogenic activity in the E-Screen

http://www.sciencedirect.com/science/article/pii/
S0960076010003572

Reproducibility of urinary phthalate metabolites in first morning urine samples

http://www.ncbi.nlm.nih.gov/pmc/articles/PMC1240840/

The 2020/2/20 Campaign: Japan Finally Standing Proud

Okinawa Rape Of A 12-year-old Japanese School Girl By Three American Blacks, see

> http://en.wikipedia.org/
> wiki/1995_Okinawa_rape_incident

On Aug. 13, 2004, a U.S. Marine Corps transport helicopter crashed onto the campus of Okinawa International University, Ginowan, injuring the three service members on board and sparking a large fire. Although the accident occurred on civilian soil, U.S. forces cordoned off the scene and blocked access to police investigators.

> http://www.japantimes.co.jp/life/2014/08/09/lifestyle/
> okinawa-pocket-resistance/

Thousands protest in Tokyo against U.S. military presence in Japan

> http://www.dailymail.co.uk/news/article-1247281/
> Thousands-protest-Tokyo-U-S-military-presence-Japan.
> html

A long-running struggle over a new military base is coming to a head

> http://www.economist.com/news/asia/21643232-long-
> running-struggle-over-new-military-base-coming-head-
> showdown

Bridgestone Stars

Tokyo Tops Paris With More Michelin Stars and Better Food

In 2007, Michelin published its first-ever restaurant guide to Tokyo and awarded the city more stars than even Paris. Jean-Luc Naret, Michelin's editorial director at the time, was emphatic: "Tokyo," he said, "was by far the world's capital of gastronomy," a comment that seemed as much an indictment of Paris, and of France, as it was a nod to Tokyo...

To illustrate the point, he mentions another fish he's using: golden eye snapper. He prefers to serve it with the skin on, but to do that, he says, he has to know the depth at which the snapper was caught; below 200 meters (655 feet), the water pressure renders the skin too tough. What I don't yet realize, but am about to discover, is that this obsessive attention to detail is nothing out of the ordinary in Tokyo. It's typical—and not just of the high-end restaurants...

> http://www.bloomberg.com/news/articles/2013-05-14/tokyo-tops-paris-with-more-michelin-stars-and-better-food

Tokyo retains title as world's food capital

> http://www.telegraph.co.uk/foodanddrink/foodanddrinknews/8923101/Tokyo-retains-title-as-worlds-food-capital.html

Japan relishes status as country with most three-starred Michelin restaurants

> http://www.telegraph.co.uk/foodanddrink/foodanddrinknews/8835949/Japan-relishes-status-as-country-with-most-three-starred-Michelin-restaurants.html

JAPANESE ULTRA-PURE FOOD 'PARADISES'

http://www.businessinsider.com/heres-what-happens-
now-that-american-farmings-fat-years-are-over-2014-12

"Japan No Country for Old Farmers as 7-Eleven Takes Plow"

http://www.bloomberg.com/news/print/2014-02-26/
japan-no-country-for-old-farmers-as-7-eleven-takes-
plow.html

JAPANESE ECONOMIC DEVELOPMENT PARTNER-
SHIPS IN 2041: A TOUR D'HORIZON

Drones Join Robots in High-Tech Future for Risky Mines

http://www.bloomberg.com/news/articles/2014-04-03/
drones-join-robots-in-high-tech-future-for-risky-mines

Japanese Team Dominates Competition to Create Generation
of Rescue Robots

http://www.nytimes.com/2013/12/23/science/japanese-
team-dominates-competition-to-create-rescue-robots.
html

ABOUT THE AUTHOR

ORIGINALLY FROM MELBOURNE, AUSTRALIA, ANDREW Blencowe discovered at an early age what it was like to live on the edge of life. During his high school years he dropped out to become a motorcycle racer. Smitten by computers in his early twenties, he went on to become founder and CEO of an international software company with offices on five continents. It is his international perspective and a drive to challenge assumptions that influence his writing interests.

Learn more at **www.AndrewBlencowe.com** including information about Blencowe's WW2 historical fiction novel *The Goddess of Fortune,* available now.